Common Wildflowers of Washington & Oregon

Common Wildflowers of Washington & Oregon

J. Duane Sept

Calypso Publishing

Copyright © 2002 J. Duane Sept

All rights reserved. No part of this publication may be reproduced, stored in a retrieval system or transmitted, in any form or by any means, without prior permission of the publisher, except by a reviewer who may quote brief passages in a review.

National Library of Canada Cataloguing in Publication Data

Sept. J. Duane, 1950-
Common wildflowers of Washington and Oregon

Includes bibliographical references and index.
ISBN 0-9730390-1-9

1. Wild flowers--Washington (State)--Identification. 2. Wild flowers--Oregon (State)--Identification. I. Title.
QK192.S46 2002   582.13'09797   C2002-910540-4

Cover photos and all other photos in this book copyright © Duane Sept

Printed and bound in Canada

Published by
Calypso Publishing
P.O. Box 1141
Sechelt, BC Canada
V0N 3A0

Website: http://www.calypso-publishing.com

Contents

Introduction 7

Natural Habitats in the Pacific Northwest............................7

Wildflower Sites in the Pacific Northwest.............................9

How to Use This Guide 10

Conservation 11

Caution 12

Wildflower & Leaf Diagrams...13

Glossary 16

Flowering Trees & Shrubs 17
       Barberry Family (Berberidaceae) 17
       Rose Family (Rosaceae) 17
       Pea Family (Fabaceae) 23
       Dogwood Family (Cornaceae) 23
       Heath Family (Ericaceae) 24
       Honeysuckle Family (Caprifoliaceae) 27
Flowering Herbs & Non-woody Plants 29
       Cattail Family (Typhaceae) 29
       Sedge Family (Cyperaceae) 30
       Arum Family (Araceae) 30
       Lily Family (Liliaceae)...................................31
       Iris Family (Iridaceae)...................................36
       Orchid Family (Orchidaceae)...............................37
       Nettle Family (Urticaceae)................................39
       Mistletoe Family (Loranthaceae)...........................40
       Buckwheat Family (Polygonaceae) 40
       Goosefoot Family (Chenopodiaceae).........................41
       Water-lily Family (Nymphaeaceae) 41
       Buttercup Family (Ranunculaceae) 42
       Barberry Family (Berberidaceae) 45
       Fumitory Family (Fumariaceae) 45

Sundew Family (Droseraceae) 46
Stonecrop Family (Crassulaceae) 46
Saxifrage Family (Saxifragaceae) 47
Rose Family (Rosaceae) 50
Pea Family (Fabaceae) 52
Geranium Family (Geraniaceae) 54
Flax Family (Linaceae) 55
Evening Primrose Family (Onagraceae) 55
Carrot Family (Apiaceae) 56
Dogwood Family (Cornaceae) 56
Wintergreen Family (Pyrolaceae) 57
Indian-pipe Family (Monotropaceae) 59
Heath Family (Ericaceae) 60
Primrose Family (Primulaceae) 61
Buckbean Family (Menyanthaceae) 62
Bindweed Family (Convolvulaceae) 62
Phlox Family (Polemoniaceae) 63
Waterleaf Family (Hydrophyllaceae) 64
Borage Family (Boraginaceae) 64
Mint Family (Lamiaceae) 65
Figwort Family (Scrophulariaceae) 66
Broomrape Family (Orobanchaceae) 68
Bladderwort Family (Lentibulariaceae) 69
Plantain Family (Plantaginaceae) 69
Valerian Family (Valerianaceae) 70
Harebell Family (Campanulaceae) 70
Aster Family (Asteraceae) 71

Additional Reading 77

Acknowledgments 78

Wildflower Checklist 79

Index 85

6

Introduction

The rich Pacific Northwest includes diverse habitats from arid grasslands to moisture-laden mountains. Wildflowers, like birds and animals, live in these varied places. The more adaptable species live in more than one type of habitat.

Wildflowers bloom throughout the flowering season beginning with a few that are often considered the first signs of spring. At low elevations, salmonberry (p. 20) is one of the first species to flower in early spring but fireweed (p. 55) does not begin to blossom until July. Flowering dates vary from one area to another as a result of differences in precipitation, temperature and latitude. Elevation also plays an important part in the flowering sequence. A species such as cow-parsnip (p. 56) may flower in June at low elevations and perhaps a month later at higher elevations.

In any natural area, one species may be producing seeds while another species is just beginning to bud. So wildflowers blossom continually from early spring to late summer. This is an important factor for vertebrates (hummingbirds) and invertebrates (butterflies, bees, etc.) that feed on nectar or the leaves of select species. Wildflowers play an important part in an ecosystem and their presence is linked to fungi, trees, birds, mammals and invertebrates. There are likely additional links we are unaware of.

Natural Habitats in the Pacific Northwest

A wide variety of natural habitats is present throughout the Pacific Northwest. Visit a completely different habitat and you will find additional wildflower species. Some of the major habitat groups include forests and grasslands as well as freshwater and saltwater wetlands. The guide notes more specific habitat requirements when necessary.

FOREST HABITATS

The tree species present in an area vary significantly with the habitat type. Shrubs and flowering herbs normally grow in the understory of the forest or at its edge. Here the wildflowers are not as obvious and may go unnoticed.

In the temperate rainforest the main species are coniferous trees, including western red cedar and western hemlock. One treasure of the understory is the western trillium (p. 31). Drier coniferous forests may include the ponderosa pine, Douglas fir or others as the primary species. A history of fire often creates older uniform stands. Western trumpet honeysuckle (p. 28) and prince's pine (p. 58) live in these drier habitats.

Deciduous forests are common in the Pacific Northwest. Balsam poplar enjoys moist areas, especially stream and river banks. Trembling aspen can form large forests. At many sites deciduous trees may accompany coniferous species to form mixed woods. Pale coral-root (p. 39) is one wildflower that lives in both deciduous and coniferous woods.

GRASSLANDS

Today, introduced annuals and grasses dominate most of the grasslands created and maintained by a history of fire. Yellow salsify (p. 71) frequently lives in this habitat but it is not restricted to it.

ALPINE AND SUBALPINE

Alpine and subalpine areas are found at elevations above the montane forest. Here a much shorter growing season severely restricts the plant species. Spreading phlox (p. 63) and western anemone (p. 42) are two wildflowers that thrive in these higher mountain environments.

FRESHWATER WETLANDS

Freshwater wetlands include rivers, creeks, streams, lakes, bogs, fens and marshes. Bogs have standing water and are high in acidity. Fens and marshes are not acidic, so the plant communities here are very different. The band of vegetation along the edges of rivers, creeks and streams is often distinct from the surrounding area. The yellow pond-lily (p. 41) and buckbean (p. 62) are two examples of species restricted to freshwater wetland environments.

SALTWATER WETLANDS

Saltwater or maritime wetlands is an example of an area with reduced numbers of flowering species. These intertidal habitats include rocky, sandy and mud shores. Seaside plantain (p. 69) is one of the few species braving this harsh environment.

Wildflower Sites in the Pacific Northwest

The list of parks and preserves below represents a small sampling of the many diverse sites where visitors can find Pacific Northwest wildflowers in their natural environment. Remember that floral displays at any single site change as seasons change. Periodic visits to the same site often bring surprising results.

BRITISH COLUMBIA

1. Manning Provincial Park
2. Pacific Rim National Park
3. Mount Revelstoke National Park
4. Yoho National Park

WASHINGTON

1. Columbia National Wildlife Refuge
2. Conboy Lake National Wildlife Refuge
3. Deception Pass State Park
4. Fields Spring State Park
5. Ridgefield National Wildlife Refuge
6. San Juan Island National Historic Park
7. Olympic National Park

OREGON
1. Oregon Dunes National Recreation Area
2. Portland Audubon Wildlife Sanctuary
3. Saddle Mountain State Park
4. Upper and Lower Table Rocks (Medford)

How to Use This Guide

This photographic guide uses a variety of information to help readers identify many of the common wildflowers found throughout the Pacific Northwest.

FAMILY
A wildflower family is a grouping of one or more genera with similar overall characteristics. All orchids, for instance, belong to the family Orchidaceae, a family that includes many genera.

WILDFLOWER NAMES
This book includes a common and a scientific name for each species. All living organisms have a scientific name comprised of two parts: first, the genus (a grouping of species with common characteristics) and second, the species. Occasionally names change as new scientific information is discovered. The most current or appropriate name is included in this book.

Common names are those used in everyday conversation. Many plants have several common names. This book uses the most widely accepted name.

ADDITIONAL NAMES
Any other common names and scientific names for the species have been included here.

DESCRIPTION

For best results, use the descriptions and photographs to identify a species. Flower descriptions accompany leaf details and plant height. Together these characteristics help us identify many common wildflowers. The photographs complement the text and aid in identification.

Wildflower colors can vary significantly so use these as a general guide in the field. Occasionally some species produce white flowers.

HABITAT

Habitat is the type of area where a species normally grows. Many species are found in more than one habitat and many also have specific moisture requirements.

NOTES

Notes accompany each species to give special information, such as additional or similar species, or traditional food, healing or medicinal uses. These are not recommendations, merely notes of past use. **Caution** is advised.

Conservation

As ever-increasing pressures are placed upon the land, it is imperative that we conserve our natural resources, including wildflowers, for the future. Instead of picking flowers, capture their beauty in other ways: Photography, drawing and painting allow people to enjoy and share wildflowers. Many people have picked or transplanted wildflowers to their home gardens and as a result many species are now endangered. Parks and preserves do not allow collecting or picking of wildflowers. Transplanted species often die because they have specific requirements a garden does not meet. Several native species are now cultivated for gardens. Check your local nursery. Let's ensure that our wildflowers are preserved for future generations.

Caution

Several poisonous plants occur throughout this region and caution is advised for those who harvest any wild plant (or parts) for consumption. Information included in the text regarding medicinal or herbal use or edibility is not meant as a recommendation, but as an historical note. If you want to eat a plant be certain you are identifying it correctly. Some species, like stinging nettle (p. 39), are also of concern. **Caution is advised**.

Checklist

A checklist allows the reader to record wildflower sightings, including flowering dates and locations..

Parts of a Wildflower

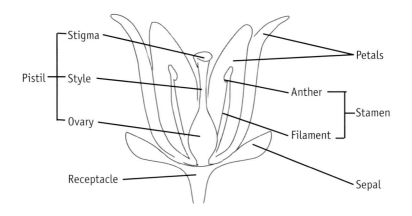

Regular Flower

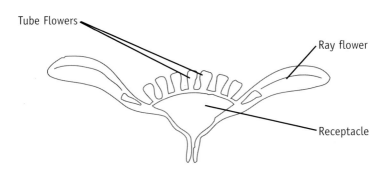

Compound Flower

Leaf Shapes

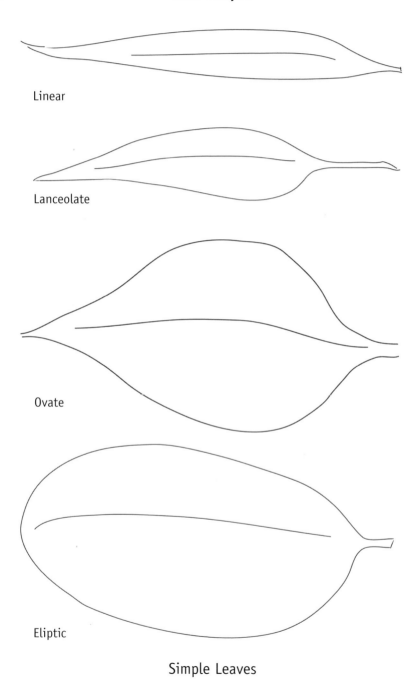

Simple Leaves

Leaf Shapes

Pinnate

Palmate

Compound Leaves

Glossary

achene: a small nut-like fruit with a single seed

anther: area of stamen where pollen is produced

annual: a plant that completes its entire life cycle in one year

basal: at the base

biennial: a plant that germinates in its first year and flowers, produces seeds and dies in its second year

bract: modified leaf found beneath a flower

bulb: modified underground stem with thick leaves (like an onion)

calyx: a structure made by the union of sepals

compound leaf: a leaf with two or more leaflets

coniferous: having reproductive organs in cones

corm: a bulb-like thickening of the stem used for storage

deciduous: a plant that looses its leaves annually

dioecious: male and female flowers are found on separate plants

disc flowers: the flowers in the aster family (usually tube-shaped)

panicle: pyramid-shaped cluster

pistil: the female reproductive structures

raceme: elongated flower stalk

ray flowers: the flattened flowers in the aster family (often marginal)

rhizome: an underground stem with buds or nodes

stigma: the tip of the pistil where pollen lands

stolon: runner with roots at the nodes

taproot: the primary root (like a carrot)

Barberry Family (Berberidaceae)

Tall Oregon-grape
Mahonia aquifolium

OTHER NAMES: Tall mahonia; also known as *Berberis aquifolium*.
DESCRIPTION: Small shrub arising from rhizomes. **Height:** To 39" (1 m) and on occasion may reach 10' (3 m). **Flowers:** Bright yellow, forms terminal clusters. **Leaves:** Leathery, shiny above with spiny teeth.
HABITAT: Open woods and rocky slopes.

The bright yellow flowers of tall Oregon-grape are as distinctive as its grape-like berries. The fruit, covered with a light-colored bloom (powder), is excellent for making juices and jellies. The yellow inner bark was once the best source for yellow dye available to aboriginal peoples. This species is the state flower of Oregon.

Rose Family (Rosaceae)

Pacific Crab Apple
Malus fusca

OTHER NAMES: Western crab apple, wild crabapple; also known as *Pyrus fusca*.
DESCRIPTION: Deciduous shrub or small tree with large spine-like spurs on branches. **Height:** To 40' (12 m). **Flowers:** White, clusters of 5-12. **Leaves:** Oval with pointed tips.
HABITAT: Wet woodlands along the coast.

The fragrant blossoms of Pacific crab apple can be found from Alaska to California. This species is well-known for its tart fruit that ranges in color from yellow to purplish-red. Although the fruit is small, it was an important food for many aboriginal peoples. It was eaten fresh or stored in a variety of ways, including under water or a mixture of water and oil to keep it fresh.

TREES & SHRUBS

Rose Family (Rosaceae)

Ocean Spray
Holodiscus discolor

OTHER NAME: Ironwood.
DESCRIPTION: Deciduous shrub. **Height:** To 12.5' (4 m). **Flowers:** Cream-colored, clustered into panicles. **Leaves:** Alternate.
HABITAT: Dry to moist open areas; low to moderate elevations.

The lofty look of ocean spray is a familiar sight to those who view it on the coast and drier areas inland. It was once known as ironwood, indicating the amazing strength and hardness of its wood, once used in construction to manufacture wooden pegs prior to the use of nails. This common shrub is found from BC to California.

Rose Family (Rosaceae)

Saskatoon
Amelanchier alnifolia

OTHER NAMES: Serviceberry, juneberry, shadbush.
DESCRIPTION: Deciduous shrub. **Height:** To 16' (5 m). **Flowers:** White, clusters of 3-20 flowers. **Leaves:** Alternate with a toothed margin.
HABITAT: Open forest, meadows and rocky areas.

Saskatoon berries are well known for their fabulous sweet taste. Aboriginal peoples gathered them in large quantities and prepared them for storage by cooking and drying into large cakes to which other berries were often added. Today saskatoons are gathered to eat fresh or to make jams, various preserves, wines and pies.

TREES & SHRUBS

Rose Family (Rosaceae)

Indian Plum

Oemlaria cerasiformis

OTHER NAMES: Osoberry; also known as *Osmaronia cerasiformis*.
DESCRIPTION: Deciduous shrub.
Height: To 16' (5 m). **Flowers:** Greenish-white, bell-shaped, clusters.
Leaves: Alternate, oblong.
HABITAT: Open forest and stream edges.

The early flowers of this fragrant shrub are one of the first signs of spring at low elevations. Its leaves smell somewhat like cucumber while its flowers have been compared to watermelon rind and cat urine, smells that certainly do not aid in convincing individuals to taste the berries of this handsome shrub. Aboriginal peoples ate the berries fresh or cooked and dried.

Rose Family (Rosaceae)

Pacific Ninebark

Physocarpus capitatus

OTHER NAME: Nine bark.
DESCRIPTION: Deciduous shrub. **Height:** To 12.5' (4 m). **Flowers:** White, numerous, small and grouped into round clusters. **Leaves:** Alternate, resemble a maple with 3-5 pointed lobes.
HABITAT: Open areas, forest edges.

The bark of Pacific ninebark is papery and often in the process of shredding. About 30 long stamens project from each flower giving the flower cluster a somewhat fuzzy appearance. Aboriginal peoples used the branches of this distinctive shrub for knitting needles and bows for children.

19

TREES & SHRUBS

Rose Family (Rosaceae)

Nootka Rose
Rosa nutkana

OTHER NAME: Common wild rose.
DESCRIPTION: Spindly shaped shrub. **Height:** To 10' (3 m). **Flowers:** Pink to deep rose, single, found at tip of branches. **Leaves:** Odd number of leaflets (normally 5 or 7), two large thorns at base of each leaf.
HABITAT: Open areas.

Several beautiful wild roses grow in the Pacific Northwest. The clustered wild rose (*Rosa pisocarpa*) is a native with clusters of beautiful, small flowers. Baldhip rose (*Rosa gymnocarpa*) drops its sepals early and as a result they are not found on its rose hips. Aboriginal people ate only the outer coverings of rose hips. They believed that eating the seeds would give a person an "itchy bottom".

Rose Family (Rosaceae)

Salmonberry
Rubus spectabilis

DESCRIPTION: Shrub rising from rhizomes. **Height:** To 12.5' (4 m). **Flowers:** Pink to reddish-purple. **Leaves:** Alternate, pinnate with three leaflets.
HABITAT: Moist forests, disturbed areas; low and medium elevations.

Salmonberry is one of the first wildflowers to bloom in spring - as early as late January in some areas. Hummingbirds often rely on this wildflower for its early nectar. This species has large, tasty, early-ripening berries. Aboriginal peoples ate both its berries and its tender shoots.

Rose Family (Rosaceae)

Thimbleberry
Rubus parviflorus

DESCRIPTION: Deciduous shrub from rhizomes.
Height: To 10' (3 m).
Flowers: White, clusters of 3-5 flowers. **Leaves:** Alternate, shaped like a maple-leaf with 3-7 lobes.
HABITAT: Open areas and clearings.

Thimbleberry flowers are delicate and showy against its large and distinctive leaves. Its sweet, tasty berries are high in Vitamin C. Unlike most of its relatives, it has few thorns. Aboriginal peoples gathered the berries for drying and ate the young sprouts as a vegetable.

Rose Family (Rosaceae)

Himalayan Blackberry
Rubus discolor

OTHER NAME: Also known as *R. procerus*.
DESCRIPTION: Shrub with stout prickles. **Length:** To 33' (10 m). **Flowers:** White to pinkish, in clusters from 5-20. **Leaves:** 3 or 5 serrated leaflets.
HABITAT: Open and disturbed sites at low elevations.

The Himalayan blackberry was imported from India and is now naturalized in much of the Pacific Northwest. It begins growing erect and then trails along the ground at an amazing rate. Blossoms from June to August become delicious berries.

TREES & SHRUBS

Rose Family (Rosaceae)

Trailing Blackberry
Rubus ursinus

OTHER NAMES: Dewberry, trailing wild blackberry, Pacific blackberry.
DESCRIPTION: Woody perennial tailing to 16' (5 m) long with curved prickles. **Height:** To 20" (50 cm). **Flowers:** White or pink, petals elongated. **Leaves:** Opposite, pinnate, 3 leaflets.
HABITAT: Disturbed sites and open forests.

This handsome shrub grows along the coast from BC through to northern California and bears sweet and juicy fruit. Its flowers are dioecious. (The male and female flowers are found on separate plants). It resembles Himalayan blackberry (p. 21) but does not grow to the same heights.

Rose Family (Rosaceae)

Pink Spiraea
Spiraea douglasii

OTHER NAMES: Hardhack, steeplebush, Douglas spiraea; formerly *S. menziesii*.
DESCRIPTION: Woody shrub. **Height:** To 79" (2 m). **Flowers:** Pink, elongated clusters of many tiny flowers. **Leaves:** Oblong and toothed.
HABITAT: Moist meadows and similar areas.

The bright floral display of pink spiraea adds a wonderful splash of color, especially where many plants grow together in profusion. It often forms an impenetrable wall that needs to be "hacked" through. This is the origin of one of its names, "hardhack". This large shrub blooms from June through July.

TREES & SHRUBS

Pea Family (Fabaceae)

Scotch Broom
Cytisus scoparius

OTHER NAME: Broom.
DESCRIPTION: Deciduous shrub.
Height: To 10' (3 m). **Flowers:** Yellow, pea-shaped. **Leaves:** Small and alternate with 3 leaflets.
HABITAT: Open areas and disturbed sites; low elevations.

Scotch broom's branches used to be tied together to make, you guessed it, brooms. The flowers make wine and during the Middle Ages the plant was also used medicinally, but beware, parts of it are **toxic**. Europeans imported Scotch broom to BC in the mid-nineteenth century and it has spread south to California and west to the Cascades.

Dogwood Family (Cornaceae)

Pacific Dogwood
Cornus nuttallii

OTHER NAMES: Flowering dogwood, western dogwood.
DESCRIPTION: Deciduous tree. **Height:** To 66' (20 m).
Flowers: Several (4-7) white petal-like bracts (modified leaves), central green cluster of flowers. **Leaves:** Oval, veins parallel the outer edge.
HABITAT: Moist forests.

Ranging from southern BC through to California this impressive tree puts on a spectacular floral display in the springtime and occasionally in the fall. Normally fall brings clusters of compact scarlet fruit. This species is the provincial flower of BC.

TREES & SHRUBS

Heath Family (Ericaceae)

Arbutus
Arbutus menziesii

OTHER NAMES: Madrone, Pacific madrone.
DESCRIPTION: A small deciduous tree that sheds its bark. **Height:** To 99' (30 m). **Flowers:** White, clusters at tips of branches. **Leaves:** Alternate, evergreen.
HABITAT: Dry, sunny, open areas.

The beautiful flowers of the arbutus accompany colorful green bark that turns bright red and sheds in the summer. Later in the season various birds relish the orange-red berries. Aboriginal peoples used arbutus in remedies for colds and stomach pains.

Heath Family (Ericaceae)

Salal
Gaultheria shallon

DESCRIPTION: Shrub. **Height:** Normally to 48" (120 cm), occasionally to 16' (5 m). **Flowers:** White or pink, urn-shaped. **Leaves:** Evergreen, leathery and shiny.
HABITAT: Coniferous forests; low to moderate elevations.

The tiny flowers of salal are a true delight to view and its fruit can be quite tasty. Aboriginal peoples dried and stored its berries for winter. Today salal is harvested for the floral industry. This species is well-known to those who frequent the forest where it can form an impressive barrier.

Heath Family (Ericaceae)

White Rhododendron

Rhododendron albiflorum

OTHER NAMES: White-flowered rhododendron, Cascades azalea.
DESCRIPTION: Shrub from rhizomes. **Height:** To 8' (2.5 m).
Flowers: White or cream-colored, cup-shaped, in clusters of 2-4. **Leaves:** Alternate with rust-colored hairs on upper surface.
HABITAT: Mountain woods.

This distinctive shrub normally grows just below treeline, but sometimes shows up as low as 800' (242 m). From southern BC to southern Oregon it lives in acid soils. The delicate flowers and the leaves are **poisonous** to children and livestock.

Heath Family (Ericaceae)

Pacific Rhododendron

Rhododendron macrophyllum

OTHER NAMES: Native rhododendron, pink rhododendron, California rhododendron, red rhododendron.
DESCRIPTION: An impressive shrub. **Height:** To 25' (8 m). **Flowers:** Pink, bell-shaped in clusters.
Leaves: Alternate, evergreen.
HABITAT: Coniferous or mixed forest; sea level to the mountains.

The spectacular display of this species highlights the flowering season in May and June even though the blossoms are short-lived. This shrub is protected in BC and is the state flower of Washington. This species has been found to be **poisonous** to livestock, especially sheep.

25

TREES & SHRUBS

Heath Family (Ericaceae)

Black Huckleberry
Vaccinium membranaceum

OTHER NAMES: Mountain huckleberry, mountain bilberry, black blueberry.
DESCRIPTION: Deciduous shrub. **Height:** To 5′ (1.5 m). **Flowers:** Pink, urn-shaped. **Leaves:** Finely toothed edges, pointed tip.
HABITAT: Coniferous forest.

Birds, bears and men find the dark purple berries of black huckleberry a tasty treat. You may agree with those who claim it is our tastiest berry. Eat the fruit raw, preserve it, or cook it in pies or muffins. Old burns often find this species especially abundant. Red huckleberry (*Vaccinium parvifolium*) is another similar species with bright red berries.

Heath Family (Ericaceae)

Bog-laurel
Kalmia microphylla

OTHER NAMES: Small bog-laurel, western bog-laurel, swamp laurel, mountain laurel; *Kalmia polifolia*.
DESCRIPTION: Short evergreen shrub from rhizomes. **Height:** To 20″ (50 cm). **Flowers:** Rose-pink, saucer-shaped forming a cluster at the tip of the plant. **Leaves:** Opposite, slender and needle-like.
HABITAT: Bogs and wet areas; low elevations to the alpine.

The small bright flowers each have ten anthers tucked into ten tiny pockets on the delicate petals to hold the petals open. When an insect touches the stamens, the miniature visitor is sprinkled with pollen. Bog-laurel contains andromedotoxin, a **poison** that causes dizziness, cramps, breathing problems and vomiting.

TREES & SHRUBS

Heath Family (Ericaceae)

Common Bearberry

Arctostaphylos uva-ursi

OTHER NAME: Kinnikinnick.
DESCRIPTION: Evergreen shrub.
Height: To 8" (20 cm). **Flowers:** Pink, urn-shaped. **Leaves:** Alternate, leathery, oval-shaped.
HABITAT: Open areas; low to alpine elevations.

Bears and small mammals such as chipmunks readily feed on the berries of this small shrub even though they are pulpy and lack in taste. Aboriginal peoples smoked the leaves and it may be that early settlers mixed the leaves with their tobacco.

Honeysuckle Family (Caprifoliaceae)

Twinflower

Linnaea borealis

OTHER NAME: Linnaea.
DESCRIPTION: Short evergreen shrub with semi-woody runners.
Height: To 4" (10 cm). **Flowers:** Pink, paired, trumpet-shaped.
Leaves: Opposite.
HABITAT: Open and closed forests, bogs and swamps.

Twinflower is a wonderfully fragrant addition to the forest floor. This tiny plant sends its spreading runners over rocks, rotting logs and moss. At times, groups of these petite flowers grace an extended area in great profusion. This circumpolar species ranges from Alaska to New Mexico.

TREES & SHRUBS

Honeysuckle Family (Caprifoliaceae)

Western Trumpet Honeysuckle

Lonicera ciliosa

OTHER NAME: Orange honeysuckle.
DESCRIPTION: Climbing vine with hollow twigs. **Height:** To 23' (7 m). **Flowers:** Orange to red, trumpet-shaped in clusters of 2-20. **Leaves:** Bright green, oval and opposite.
HABITAT: Dry open forests.

The western trumpet honeysuckle is one of the few vines found in the Pacific Northwest. It relies on larger, taller plants to anchor itself, twisting its way up toward more light in the forest canopy. As with many red flowers, this species is a favorite of hummingbirds.

Honeysuckle Family (Caprifoliaceae)

Bracted Honeysuckle

Lonicera involucrata

OTHER NAMES: Black twinberry, bearberry honeysuckle, fly honeysuckle.
DESCRIPTION: Deciduous shrub. **Height:** To 10' (3 m). **Flowers:** Yellow with dark red bracts, tubular. **Leaves:** Opposite, elliptic.
HABITAT: Moist to wet sites, forest areas.

Hummingbirds feed on the nectar and butterfly larvae feed on the leaves of this distinctive shrub. A wide variety of birds nest in its branches and the shiny black berries provide food for various creatures including the hermit thrush, robin and pine grosbeak. But beware as the fruit is **poisonous** to humans.

TREES & SHRUBS

Honeysuckle Family (Caprifoliaceae)

Red Elderberry
Sambucus racemosa

DESCRIPTION: Deciduous shrub that is foul-smelling. **Height:** To 10′ (3 m). **Flowers:** Creamy white, small in clusters. **Leaves:** Compound (pinnate), 5-7 leaflets.
HABITAT: Moist areas, open forest.

Two varieties of elderberry can be found in the Pacific Northwest. Red elderberry (*Sambucus racemosa* var. *pubens*) and black elderberry (*Sambucus racemosa* var. *melancapra*) are distinguished by the different colors of their fruit. Their berries are often mixed with other species' to make jams, jellies, pies and wines.

HERBS (NON-WOODY PLANTS)

Cattail Family (Typhaceae)

Common Cattail
Typha latifolia

OTHER NAMES: Cattail, broad-leaved cattail.
DESCRIPTION: Aquatic perennial from rhizomes. **Height:** To 10′ (3 m). **Flowers:** Green changing to brown, distinctive cylindrical spike. **Leaves:** Elongated.
HABITAT: Quiet and slow moving fresh water.

"The supermarket of the swamp," the common cattail, which grows in profusion along the edge of marshes and ponds, has many uses: Ground roots and pollen make flour. Boiled young flower stalks are eaten like corn. Down from mature seeds makes excellent fire tinder or pillow stuffing. Leaves are good weaving material.

HERBS

Sedge Family (Cyperaceae)

Many-spiked Cottongrass

Eriophorum angustifolium

OTHER NAMES: Tall cottongrass, narrow-leaved cottongrass; also known as *E. polystachion*.
DESCRIPTION: Perennial sedge from rhizomes. **Height:** To 32" (80 cm). **Fruit:** White, elongated bristles in clusters, two or more fruiting heads per plant.
Leaves: Basal, triangular, channelled near tip.
HABITAT: Wet meadows.

Many-spiked cottongrass is a sedge rather than a grass. Sedges have solid, triangular stems when viewed in cross-section. In favorable habitats the seed heads of this species often transform an area into a "sea of cotton".

Arum Family (Araceae)

Skunk Cabbage

Lysichiton americanus

OTHER NAMES: Western skunk cabbage, swamp lantern, yellow arum; also known as *Lysichitum americanum*.
DESCRIPTION: Perennial. **Height:** To 5' (1.5 m). **Flowers:** Greenish-yellow, arranged on a central axis with a single large bract. **Leaves:** Basal, oval-shaped.
HABITAT: Swamps, wet meadows and similar sites.

Skunk cabbage is a colorful addition to wet areas in the spring and a favorite food for both the black bear and grizzly. It was also a famine food for aboriginal peoples. This robust species thrives from Alaska to California. Despite its name, it does not smell like a skunk. It has its own distinctive odor.

HERBS

Lily Family (Liliaceae)

False Solomon's Seal
Maianthemum racemosum

OTHER NAMES: False spikenard; *Smilacina racemosa*.
DESCRIPTION: Perennial from rhizomes.
Height: To 39" (1 m). **Flowers:** White, on a terminal cluster. **Leaves:** Alternate, elliptical with parallel veins.
HABITAT: Moist forests; low to subalpine elevations.

This delightful tall species is found throughout much of North America. Its weight often pulls it down to grow somewhat horizontally. A close look at a cluster of these delicate flowers reveals its tiny lily-shaped flowers. Delicate red berries add a pleasant touch of color once its flowers have passed.

Lily Family (Liliaceae)

Western Trillium
Trillium ovatum

OTHER NAME: Wake robin.
DESCRIPTION: Perennial from a short rhizome. **Height:** To 18" (45 cm). **Flowers:** White, 3 petals and 3 sepals on a stalk. **Leaves:** In whorls.
HABITAT: Moist or wet forests or shaded areas; low to middle elevations.

Western trillium, also known as wake robin, is commonly seen from March to May when the familiar American robin returns in spring. Ants often drag the seeds back to their nests where they feed on the outer covering. Then they discard the seeds, which are free to grow in the new location. Ants also disperse Pacific bleeding heart seeds (p. 45).

HERBS

Lily Family (Liliaceae)

False Lily-of-the-valley

Maianthemum dilatatum

OTHER NAMES: Two-leaved false lily-of-the-valley, two-leaved Solomon's seal, deerberry.
DESCRIPTION: Perennial from a creeping rhizome.
Height: To 16" (40 cm).
Flowers: White, elongated cluster of small flowers. **Leaves:** Alternate, 1-3 heart-shaped.
HABITAT: Moist shady forests and wet areas.

False lily-of-the-valley is a common species that carpets forest floors from Alaska to California. Aboriginal peoples used this delightful plant to treat many ailments, including sterility, sore eyes, cuts and internal injuries. The berries were also eaten but not highly regarded as food.

Lily Family (Liliaceae)

Queen's Cup

Clintonia uniflora

OTHER NAMES: One-flowered clintonia, blue-bead, bead lily, corn-lily.
DESCRIPTION: Perennial herb from creeping rhizomes.
Height: To 6" (15 cm).
Flowers: White, solitary with narrow petals. **Leaves:** Basal.
HABITAT: Moist forests, shaded sites; low to high elevations.

Queen's cup is a delicate, solitary flower that is eventually replaced with a distinctive, single blue berry. Grouse are thought to feed on these berries while aboriginal peoples used them to make a stain or dye. This species grows from Alaska to California.

HERBS

Lily Family (Liliaceae)

White Fawn Lily

Erythronium oregonum

OTHER NAMES: Easter lily, white trout lily.
DESCRIPTION: Perennial herb from a corm.
Height: To 6" (15 cm).
Flowers: White tepals (sepals or petals) are bent backwards. **Leaves:** Paired at the base.
HABITAT: Woodlands, rocky crevices and grasslands.

The white fawn lily is a striking wildflower that needs to be protected since its numbers have been drastically reduced in the face of development. Do not pick this flower; the plant cannot survive without it. This large and beautiful species, like several other native wildflowers, has been extensively picked and is no longer found in many of its former haunts.

Lily Family (Liliaceae)

Nodding Onion

Allium cernuum

DESCRIPTION: Perennial from a bulb.
Height: To 20" (50 cm). **Flowers:** Pink to purple, hanging umbrella-like cluster. **Leaves:** Long and grass-like.
HABITAT: Dry exposed grassy areas and open woods.

You could easily miss seeing the nodding onion when it is not in bloom, but the scent will give it away. The sweet onion taste of the bulbs and leaves enhanced the diet of aboriginal peoples. A word of **caution** to those harvesting nodding onion bulbs: The bulbs of meadow death-camas (p. 34) look very similar but are **deadly**.

Flower color and shape are distinctive.

HERBS

Lily Family (Liliaceae)

Fool's Onion

Triteleia hyacinthina

OTHER NAMES: White triteleia; also known as *Brodiaea hyacinthina*.
DESCRIPTION: Perennial from a corm. **Height:** To 28" (70 cm). **Flowers:** White with a blue or green mid-vein, clustered at tip of stem. **Leaves:** Grass-like, basal.
HABITAT: Open meadows, grassy areas.

Fool's onion looks like an onion but lacks the distinctive odor and taste. This species grows from southern BC to California, often in the company of nodding onion (p. 33).

Lily Family (Liliaceae)

Meadow Death-camas

Zygadenus venenosus

OTHER NAMES: Death camas, poison camas.
DESCRIPTION: Perennial from a bulb with black scales. **Height:** To 24" (60 cm). **Flowers:** Creamy-white, tiny, tightly clustered. **Leaves:** Basal, grass-like.
HABITAT: Open meadows, forest edges and open forests.

As its common name suggests, meadow death-camas is **deadly poisonous**. The bulbs contain powerful alkaloids and are easily confused with the bulbs of common camas (*Camassia quamash*), a species with edible bulbs and blue flowers. Flower color will distinguish these species.

HERBS

Lily Family (Liliaceae)

Chocolate Lily

Fritillaria lanceolata

OTHER NAMES: Mission bell, rice-root, Indian rice, checker lily, skunk lily.
DESCRIPTION: Perennial from a bulb. **Height:** To 32" (80 cm). **Flowers:** Brown mottled with greenish-yellow, single to clusters of 5. **Leaves:** Lanceolate, in whorls of 3-5.
HABITAT: Open woodlands, wet meadows; sea level to sub-alpine elevations.

Alas, the chocolate lily's name derives from its color and not its taste, even though the bulb and bulblets, that resemble cooked white rice, were an important food source for aboriginal peoples from southern BC to California.

Lily Family (Liliaceae)

Tiger Lily

Lilium columbianum

OTHER NAMES: Columbia lily, Oregon lily.
DESCRIPTION: Perennial from a white bulb. **Height:** To 47" (1.2 m). **Flowers:** Orange with purple to deep red spots in the center, one to many flowers on one plant. **Leaves:** In whorls, lanceolate.
HABITAT: Open forests and meadows.

This species' common name likely originates from the spots on its showy flowers. One folk tale includes a belief that those who can smell the tiger lily will acquire freckles. At one time the bulbs of the tiger lily were boiled or steamed and used as a food.

HERBS

Lily Family (Liliaceae)

Beargrass

Xerophyllum tenax

OTHER NAME: Sometimes misspelled *Zerophyllum*.
DESCRIPTION: Perennial herb from short rhizomes. **Height:** To 5' (1.5 m). **Flowers:** White, tiny, terminal cluster. **Leaves:** Basal, grass-like.
HABITAT: Open meadows, forest; low elevations to subalpine.

The striking floral display of beargrass follows an irregular schedule. Thousands of plants bloom together in great profusion every 3-10 years. This distinctive wildflower is seldom confused with other species. It provides food for rodents, deer, elk, bighorn sheep and bear.

Iris Family (Iridaceae)

Yellow-flag

Iris pseudacorus

OTHER NAME: Yellow flag.
DESCRIPTION: Perennial herb from a creeping rhizome. **Height:** To 36" (90 cm). **Flowers:** Bright yellow, occasionally cream-colored. **Leaves:** Elongated and stalkless.
HABITAT: Ditches, stream edges and similar sites.

Introduced from Europe, yellow-flag now grows in southern BC and Washington. The extended floral display lasts from April through August. This species was formerly used for a variety of herbal remedies; a sliced rhizome rubbed on a sore tooth was said to relieve the pain.

HERBS

Orchid Family (Orchidaceae)

Fairyslipper
Calypso bulbosa

OTHER NAMES: Venus' slipper, calypso orchid, pink slipper orchid, false ladyslipper.
DESCRIPTION: Perennial herb. **Height:** To 8" (20 cm). **Flowers:** Rose-purple with purple streaks on the slipper-like lower lip, a beard-like tuft is also present on this lip. **Leaves:** Basal, solitary.
HABITAT: Coniferous forests; from low to moderate elevations.

This orchid's scientific name comes from the goddess Calypso and the flower is certainly goddess-like. Fairyslipper is widespread and grows in a variety of forest situations rich in leaf litter. Picking and trampling have reduced the number of fairyslippers. Take care not to exterminate this species.

Orchid Family (Orchidaceae)

Mountain Ladyslipper
Cypripedium montanum

OTHER NAMES: Moccasin flower, white lady's slipper.
DESCRIPTION: Perennial herb. **Height:** To 28" (70 cm). **Flowers:** White with purplish veins, lip is shaped into a large pouch. **Leaves:** Egg-shaped, attached to central stalk.
HABITAT: Dry and moist open forests.

The flamboyant mountain ladyslipper sports elongated petals and copper-colored sepals. This rare and fragrant species is reserved for those who experience mountains from BC to California. The mountain ladyslipper grows so slowly it takes up to 15 years to flower. Do not pick this elegant species. It is threatened.

HERBS

Orchid Family (Orchidaceae)

Spotted Coralroot
Corallorhiza maculata

DESCRIPTION:
Saprophyte from rhizomes. **Height:** To 12" (30 cm). **Flowers:** Reddish-purple to white with purple spots on lip, loose terminal cluster. **Leaves:** Thin sheaths on stem.
HABITAT: Coniferous and mixed forests.

The elegant flowers of the coralroot orchids are a pleasant addition to any forest. The plants lack green leaves and as a result cannot photosynthesize. Instead, they obtain their nutrients from decaying organic material in the soil, through fungi also living in the soil.

Orchid Family (Orchidaceae)

Striped Coralroot
Corallorhiza striata

OTHER NAMES: Striped coral-root, madder-stripes.
DESCRIPTION: Saprophyte from rhizomes. **Height:** To 16" (40 cm).
Flowers: Pink to yellowish pink, sepals striped with purple, loose terminal cluster. **Leaves:** Thin sheaths on stem.
HABITAT: Coniferous and mixed forests.

Striped coralroot is a handsome orchid blooming from April to August. It grows randomly throughout the Pacific Northwest. Coralroot orchids get their name from their coral-like rhizomes.

HERBS

Orchid Family (Orchidaceae)

Pale Coralroot
Corallorhiza trifida

OTHER NAMES: Yellow coralroot, northern coralroot.
DESCRIPTION: Saprophyte from rhizomes. **Height:** To 10" (25 cm). **Flowers:** Greenish-yellow to white, occasionally with faint red spots, loose terminal cluster. **Leaves:** Thin sheaths on stem.
HABITAT: Coniferous or deciduous forests.

Pale coralroot, like all coralroots, grows in the shaded forests of the Pacific Northwest. This species, however, is found inland rather than along the coast. Although this species sometimes flowers with fairyslipper (p. 37) in early spring, it can bloom as late as August.

Nettle Family (Urticaceae)

Stinging Nettle
Urtica dioica

OTHER NAMES: Indian spinach, northwest nettle.
DESCRIPTION: Perennial from spreading rhizomes. **Height:** To 10' (3 m). **Flowers:** Green, very small, elongated clusters hang downward. **Leaves:** Opposite, oval or heart-shaped.
HABITAT: Moist meadows, open forest, disturbed sites.

Each stinging nettle flower spike is a cluster of either male or female flowers. The stiff, hollow hairs arming leaves and stems contain formic acid, a strong irritant to the skin. If you break these hairs, the acid will cause a rash and blisters. Surprisingly, you can eat the cooked young leaves and stems.

HERBS

Mistletoe Family (Loranthaceae)

American Dwarf Mistletoe

Arceuthobium americanum

OTHER NAME: Dwarf mistletoe.
DESCRIPTION: Parasitic shrub that grows on pines. **Height:** Normally to 2 1/4" (6 cm) and occasionally to 4" (10 cm).
Flowers: Greenish-yellow, tiny.
Leaves: Opposite, reduced to minute scales.
HABITAT: Pine forests, normally on lodgepole pine.

American dwarf mistletoe produces a pronounced change to the normal growth pattern of their host tree, creating a "witch's broom." Several species occur in the Pacific Northwest where they can be often identified by their hosts. Christmas mistletoe (*Phoradendron flavescens*) is a popular relative.

Buckwheat Family (Polygonaceae)

Water Smartweed

Polygonum amphibium

OTHER NAME: Ladysthumb.
DESCRIPTION: Aquatic perennial.
Length: To 39" (1 m). **Flowers:** Deep-pink, dense terminal spike.
Leaves: Alternate, elliptical to oblong.
HABITAT: In freshwater or at its edge.

On every continent except Australia, the numerous flowers of this brightly colored species provide a spectacle while floating on water or at its wet edge. This attractive species provides food for a variety of wildlife including waterfowl, shorebirds and muskrats.

40

HERBS

Goosefoot Family (Chenopodiaceae)

Strawberry Blight

Chenopodium capitatum

OTHER NAME: Indian plant.
DESCRIPTION: Annual herb from a taproot.
Height: To 20" (50 cm). **Flowers:** Green, dense, round clusters. **Fruit:** Bright crimson, fleshy. **Leaves:** Alternate, spear-shaped.
HABITAT: Open sites.

Although commonly thought to be imported from Europe, strawberry blight is native to North America and was introduced to Europe in the seventeenth century. Aboriginal peoples used the bright red fruit for dye. People can eat young plants raw or cooked in a variety of dishes.

Water-lily Family (Nymphaeaceae)

Yellow Pond-lily

Nuphar polysepalum

OTHER NAMES: Yellow water lily, spatterdock, cow-lily; *N. luteum*.
DESCRIPTION: Aquatic perennial from extensive rhizomes.
Height: To 79" (2 m). **Flowers:** Yellow, cup-shaped, waxy.
Leaves: Heart-shaped with long stems.
HABITAT: Ponds, small lakes and similar quiet waters.

This aquatic species is common throughout much of the Pacific Northwest. Aboriginal peoples used the rhizomes to combat tuberculosis and other diseases and included the seeds in their diets. The fragrant waterlily (*Nymphaea odorata*) is a similar species with white flowers, introduced from eastern North America.

HERBS

Buttercup Family (Ranunculaceae)

Western Anemone

Anemone occidentalis

OTHER NAMES: Western pasque flower, chalice flower, tow-headed baby, moptop.
DESCRIPTION: Hairy perennial herb from a taproot. **Height:** To 12" (30 cm). **Flowers:** White, solitary. **Leaves:** Stem and basal, finely dissected.
HABITAT: Open meadows; subalpine and alpine.

From northern BC through to California, when the snow melts in the alpine and subalpine, the western anemone begins its spectacular floral display. The large saucer-shaped flowers range in color from a pale cream to white with just a hint of blue. Soon after the flowers have finished, the moptops (seed heads) take over and a second show begins.

Buttercup Family (Ranunculaceae)

Mountain Marsh-marigold

Caltha leptosepala

OTHER NAMES: Alpine white marsh-marigold, elkslip.
DESCRIPTION: Perennial herb from rhizomes. **Height:** To 16" (40 cm). **Flowers:** Sepals white occasionally tinged with blue, center yellow, saucer-shaped. **Leaves:** Basal, heart-shaped, waxy.
HABITAT: Wet open meadows.

Mountain marsh-marigold blooms so early in the season it often pushes its way through the last remnants of snow at higher elevations. Some say this handsome species is edible after it is boiled, while at least one authority states that it contains **poisonous** compounds. Caution is advised.

HERBS

Buttercup Family (Ranunculaceae)

Tall Buttercup
Ranunculus acris

OTHER NAME: Meadow buttercup.
DESCRIPTION: Hairy perennial with fibrous roots. **Height:** To 32" (80 cm). **Flowers:** Bright yellow, saucer-shaped. **Leaves:** Deeply divided and appear to be 5 lobed.
HABITAT: Moist meadows, roadsides and disturbed areas.

Many species of buttercup grow in the Pacific Northwest. Tall buttercup, introduced from Europe, spread rapidly between Alaska and California. Another similar species, creeping buttercup (*Ranunculus repens*), is one of the easiest to identify with stolons (runners) that root at the nodes.

Buttercup Family (Ranunculaceae)

Baneberry
Actaea rubra

OTHER NAME: Red baneberry.
DESCRIPTION: Perennial from rhizomes. **Height:** To 39" (1 m). **Flowers:** White, clustered on elongated stalks. **Leaves:** Alternate, compound.
HABITAT: Open forest.

Shiny white or red berries follow the delicate white flower clusters of baneberry. **Beware!** This whole plant is **very poisonous**. It was once believed that the red and white berries belonged to different species. Scientists now know, however, that they are merely two color forms of the same species.

43

HERBS

Buttercup Family (Ranunculaceae)

Blue Clematis
Clematis occidentalis

OTHER NAMES: Blue virgin's bower; *Clematis verticillaris*.
DESCRIPTION: Perennial vine. **Height:** To 16' (5 m).
Flowers: Showy purple to blue sepals. **Leaves:** Compound with three leaflets.
HABITAT: Moist and dry woodlands.

Blue Clematis often goes unnoticed until May and June when the distinctive flowers appear. These begin like hanging lanterns and become delicate mops of feathery achenes. The seed heads appear as silvery globes when touched with sunlight as the vines reach for the forest canopy.

Buttercup Family (Ranunculaceae)

Red Columbine
Aquilegia formosa

OTHER NAMES: Western columbine, Sitka columbine.
DESCRIPTION: Perennial from a taproot. **Height:** To 39" (1 m).
Flowers: Red sepals, 5 red spurs surround the central yellow stamens and styles.
Leaves: Basal.
HABITAT: Moist open meadows, forest edges, roadsides and beaches; coast to timberline.

From June to August this impressive wildflower's nectar and bright colors attract butterflies and hummingbirds. Aboriginal people used this plant as a remedy for ailments like dizziness, diarrhea and aching joints. Yellow columbine (*Aquilegia flavescens*), is a similar species with yellow sepals.

HERBS

Barberry Family (Berberidaceae)

Vanilla Leaf
Achlys triphylla

OTHER NAMES: May-leaf, sweet-after-death, deer-foot.
DESCRIPTION: Perennial from rhizomes. **Height:** To 14" (35 cm). **Flowers:** White, clustered into a spike. **Leaves:** Broad, large and divided into 3 leaflets.
HABITAT: Moist, shady woods.

This delicate wildflower is comprised only of stamens; it lacks both petals and sepals. Large, broad leaves dwarf the blossoms of this shade-loving species. Vanilla leaf can often be found in great profusion from southern BC to northern California.

Fumitory Family (Fumariaceae)

Pacific Bleeding Heart
Dicentra formosa

OTHER NAME: Western bleeding heart.
DESCRIPTION: Perennial from rhizomes. **Height:** To 20" (50 cm). **Flowers:** Purple-pink, heart-shaped, form a cluster at top of plant. **Leaves:** Celery-like.
HABITAT: Moist open woods and stream banks.

Formosa means beautiful in Latin and from BC to California this beautiful, fragrant species blossoms from March to July. The delicate flower of Pacific bleeding heart is easy to identify and makes an attractive addition to the garden.

HERBS

Sundew Family (Droraceae)

Round-leaved Sundew

Drosera rotundifolia

DESCRIPTION: Insectivorous perennial from rhizomes. **Height:** To 7" (18 cm). **Flowers:** White, opens in full sunlight. **Leaves:** Basal, rounded ends with glandular hairs.
HABITAT: Sphagnum bogs and fens.

This remarkable plant has interesting feeding habits. Droplets of glue-like sap at the ends of tiny hairs on the leaves lay in wait. When an insect alights on one glue-tipped hair, additional hairs slowly lean to touch the insect so it cannot escape. Then the round-leaf sundew absorbs nutrients from the helpless intruder.

Stonecrop Family (Crassulaceae)

Broad-leaved Stonecrop

Sedum spathulifolium

OTHER NAME: Broadleaf stonecrop.
DESCRIPTION: Perennial from rhizomes. **Height:** To 8" (20 cm). **Flowers:** Yellow, clustered. **Leaves:** Alternate, flattened and wider at the ends.
HABITAT: Cliffs and rocky areas.

Broad-leaved stonecrop is one of several species of colorful stonecrops found in the area. Oregon stonecrop (*Sedum oreganum*) displays fleshy, spoon-shaped leaves reminiscent of a succulent. The leaves of another species, the lance-leaved stonecrop (*Sedum lanceolatum*), are rounded and lanceolate.

HERBS

Stonecrop Family (Crassulaceae)

Roseroot

Sedum integrifolium

OTHER NAME: Also known as *S. rosea*.
DESCRIPTION: Succulent perennial from branched rhizomes. **Height:** To 8" (20 cm). **Flowers:** Dark purple to pink, clustered at top of plant.
Leaves: Green or pink, fleshy, oval, alternate.
HABITAT: Rocky sites.

The impressive roseroot, which lives from Alaska to California, emits a distinctive rose-like fragrance when its rhizome is cut or bruised. Aboriginal peoples ate the young shoots and succulent leaves that are high in Vitamins A and C.

Saxifrage Family (Saxifragaceae)

Common Mitrewort

Mitella nuda

OTHER NAMES: Bare-stemmed mitrewort, bishop's cap.
DESCRIPTION: Perennial from rhizomes. **Height:** To 8" (20 cm). **Flowers:** Greenish-yellow, antennae-like petals, 10 stamens. **Leaves:** Heart or kidney-shaped.
HABITAT: Moist forests and wet areas.

If you want to truly appreciate common mitrewort, take a close look at the small flowers. It is one of several plants that employ splash-cup dispersal in which raindrops hit ripe capsules to eject the tiny seeds. The mitreworts in the Pacific Northwest have either 5 or 10 stamens. This species is the only one with 10.

Saxifrage Family (Saxifragaceae)

Small-flowered Alumroot

Heuchera micrantha

OTHER NAME: Alum root.
DESCRIPTION: Perennial herb from rhizomes. **Height:** To 24" (60 cm). **Flowers:** White, arranged in an elongated cluster. **Leaves:** Basal, hairy, longer than wide.
HABITAT: Rocky crevices, stream banks and similar situations; sea level to subalpine.

Small-flowered alumroot is a delight to find, especially in a picturesque location among rocks beside the water. It is one of several similar species found in the area; its distinctive leaves aid in identification. The range of this delicate species extends from northern BC to California.

Saxifrage Family (Saxifragaceae)

Tall Fringecup

Tellima grandiflora

OTHER NAME: Fringecup.
DESCRIPTION: Perennial from rhizomes. **Height:** To 32" (80 cm). **Flowers:** Greenish-white to pink, petals frilled, 10 stamens, loose clusters. **Leaves:** Basal, heart-shaped.
HABITAT: Moist forests, stream edges.

Tall fringecup is a common herb that ranges from Alaska to California in forests of low to middle elevations. Aboriginal peoples used a tea made from this fragrant plant to increase their appetite. Elves are said to eat this species to improve their night vision.

HERBS

Saxifrage Family (Saxifragaceae)

Foamflower

Tiarella trifoliata

OTHER NAMES: False mitrewort, lace flower; includes *T. laciniata*, *T. unifoliata*.
DESCRIPTION: Perennial from a short rhizome.
Height: To 24" (60 cm). **Flowers:** White, very small and scattered in an elongated cluster.
Leaves: Basal, 3 leaflets or 3 lobes on a single leaf.
HABITAT: Moist areas, coniferous forest.

Don't miss the delicate beauty of the foamflower that grows on the forest floor. A hand lens or magnifying glass reveals long stamens protruding from the petals of the small flowers. A 10X magnifying lens is an excellent tool to view, identify and truly appreciate the beauty and design of many wildflowers.

Saxifrage Family (Saxifragaceae)

Fringed Grass-of-parnassus

Parnassia fimbriata

DESCRIPTION: Perennial herb from rhizomes.
Height: To 12" (30 cm).
Flowers: White, fringed along the lower petal edges, solitary. **Leaves:** Basal, kidney-shaped.
HABITAT: Moist meadows, bogs and fens.

Fringed grass-of-parnassus is a moisture-loving member of the saxifrage family rather than a grass. The elongated stem supporting the flower is the only part of this delicate species that resembles a grass. Five sterile yellow stamens alternate with five fertile stamens.

HERBS

Rose Family (Rosaceae)

Goat's Beard
Aruncus dioicus

OTHER NAMES: Goatsbeard, spaghetti flower; also known as *Aruncus sylvester*.
DESCRIPTION: Perennial from rhizomes base. **Height:** To 79" (2 m). **Flowers:** Tiny white flowers are shaped into elongated clusters. **Leaves:** Large, compound.
HABITAT: Moist woodlands.

In June and July male and female blossoms appear on separate plants of this large and seemingly unmanageable wildflower. Aboriginal peoples used this plant to remedy various ailments: smallpox, colds, sore throats, gonorrhea and tuberculosis.

Rose Family (Rosaceae)

Wild Strawberry
Fragaria virginiana

OTHER NAMES: Virginia strawberry; also known as *F. glauca*.
DESCRIPTION: Perennial from rhizomes with several runners. **Height:** To 6" (15 cm). **Flowers:** White, saucer-shaped. **Leaves:** Comprised of 3 leaflets, end tooth on tip is shorter and narrower than the neighbouring teeth.
HABITAT: Open, well-drained sites.

The fabulous fruit of the strawberry needs no introduction. Wild strawberry plants provided the major part of the gene pool necessary to develop the domestic varieties we now grow in the garden. Other similar native strawberries include the wood strawberry (*F. vesca*) that has yellowish leaves and the coastal strawberry (*F. chiloensis*) with its thick leathery leaves. The coastal strawberry is never far from the ocean.

HERBS

Rose Family (Rosaceae)

Large-leaved Avens

Geum macrophyllum

OTHER NAME: Big-leaved avens.
DESCRIPTION: Perennial herb from rhizomes. **Height:** To 39" (1 m).
Flowers: Bright yellow, widely spaced, saucer-shaped petals.
Leaves: Basal, large, 3 or more segments, end segment much larger than the rest.
HABITAT: Moist woods and openings; low elevations to subalpine meadows.

Ranging from Alaska to California, the large-leaved avens hitches a ride on mammal fur or human clothing by attaching its hooked seeds to moving hosts. Aboriginal peoples used this plant as a contraceptive and to treat rheumatism.

Rose Family (Rosaceae)

Old Man's Whiskers

Geum triflorum

OTHER NAMES: Prairie smoke, three-flowered avens, purple avens.
DESCRIPTION: Perennial herb from a rhizome. **Height:** To 16" (40 cm). **Flowers:** Purple, grouped in 3's, urn-shaped on drooping stalks.
Leaves: Basal, fern-like.
HABITAT: Dry and open areas.

The wonderful names of this common species are a tribute to man's imagination. After this species has finished flowering early in the spring, it produces very distinctive seed heads. A single feathery achene resembles an elderly man's beard while a field of these seed heads appears somewhat like smoke in a breeze.

HERBS

Pea Family (Fabaceae)

Beach Pea

Lathyrus japonicus

OTHER NAME: Also known as *L. maritimus*.
DESCRIPTION: Perennial herb from rhizomes.
Height: To 5' (1.5 m) high or trailing. **Flowers:** Reddish-purple to light blue, pea-shaped. **Leaves:** Compound with 6-12 leaflets.
HABITAT: Coastal beaches.

Several attractive members of the pea family grow in the Pacific Northwest. Coiled terminal tendrils anchor the beach pea to its environment. Later in the season hairy pods produce seeds said to be edible. Many species of the pea family are **poisonous**, however, and **caution** is advised.

Pea Family (Fabaceae)

Tufted Vetch

Vicia cracca

OTHER NAMES: Cow vetch, bird vetch.
DESCRIPTION: Perennial herb with climbing stems. **Height:** To 79" (2 m).
Flowers: Reddish-purple to blue, pea-like, 20-50 flowers along one side.
Leaves: Compound with 16-24 leaflets and branched tendrils.
HABITAT: Open areas; low to moderate elevations.

Tufted vetch, an elegant species introduced from Eurasia, is common over much of North America. Another similar introduced species, the wooly vetch (*Vicia villosa*), graces disturbed sites with two-toned flowers. As its name suggests, it is very hairy.

HERBS

Pea Family (Fabaceae)

Arctic Lupine
Lupinus arcticus

OTHER NAMES: Subalpine broad-leaved lupine; also known as *L. latifolius*.
DESCRIPTION: Perennial from rhizomes. **Height:** To 24″ (60 cm). **Flowers:** Blue, pea-like, arranged in a spike-like raceme or cluster. **Leaves:** Basal, long stalked, 6-8 leaflets.
HABITAT: Moist, open meadows and similar situations; moderate to alpine elevations.

Arctic lupine puts on a wonderful display of color at moist sites. Although more common at high elevations, it also can be found at lower sites. Several other lupines also grow in the area including large-leaved lupine (*Lupinus polyphyllus*) that can reach 5′ (1.5 m) tall. It sports 10 to 17 leaflets on its large leaves.

Pea Family (Fabaceae)

Red Clover
Trifolium pratense

OTHER NAMES: Purple clover, peavine clover, cowgrass.
DESCRIPTION: Perennial from a taproot. **Height:** To 32″ (80 cm). **Flowers:** Red to deep pink, sepals fused into a tube and clustered into a dense head. **Leaves:** 3 leaflets, immediately below flowers.
HABITAT: Open fields and agricultural areas.

Red clover is a short-lived perennial introduced from Europe. Two other species also inhabit the Pacific Northwest: White clover (*Trifolium repens*) sprawls low on the ground. Alsike clover (*Trifolium hybridum*) stands erect with its light pink flower heads.

HERBS

Geranium Family (Geraniaceae)

Herb Robert
Geranium robertianum

OTHER NAMES: Robert geraniium, stinky geranium, stinky bob.
DESCRIPTION: Annual from a taproot. **Height:** To 24" (60 cm). **Flowers:** Pink to reddish-purple, sepals hairy. **Leaves:** Celery-like, deeply divided, red stems.
HABITAT: Open woods, rocky areas.

This common species was introduced from Europe and can now be found from southern BC to California. Herb Robert was possibly named after Robin Goodfellow, who was also known as Robin Hood. This plant has a strong and distinctive smell and begins blooming in April.

Geranium Family (Geraniaceae)

Sticky Purple Geranium
Geranium viscosissimum

OTHER NAMES: Sticky geranium, sticky purple cranesbill.
DESCRIPTION: Perennial herb from a woody base. **Height:** To 36" (90 cm). **Flowers:** Pink to magenta with deep purple veins, saucer-shaped. **Leaves:** Primarily basal, palmate with 5-7 lobes.
HABITAT: Open areas, forest edge.

The sticky hairs covering much of this plant protect it from insects. As this species matures the fruit capsule dries and splits open. The recoil is so forceful seeds are projected several feet away. This species is sometimes called cranesbill because its style is shaped like the bill of a stork or crane.

54

HERBS

Flax Family (Linaceae)

Western Blue Flax
Linum lewisii

OTHER NAMES: Wild blue flax; also known as *Linum perenne*.
DESCRIPTION: Perennial herb from a woody root. **Height:** To 28" (70 cm). **Flowers:** Blue, saucer-shaped. **Leaves:** Alternate, linear.
HABITAT: Dry open areas; grassland to subalpine areas.

The handsome western blue flax quivers with the slightest breeze on its slender wiry stems. Aboriginal peoples used the long stringy fibers found in the stems to make thread, fishing line and nets. This species grows throughout much of North America.

Evening Primrose Family (Onagraceae)

Fireweed
Epilobium angustifolium

OTHER NAMES: Great willowherb, willow-herb.
DESCRIPTION: Perennial from its rhizome-like root. **Height:** To 10' (3 m). **Flowers:** Rose to purple, arranged in a terminal cluster. **Leaves:** Alternate and lance-shaped.
HABITAT: Open forest areas, forest edges, roadsides and burned areas.

A spectacular display is produced when this species colonizes new areas, especially burned sites. Fireweed flowers from July to September and its range extends from Alaska to California. It is high in Vitamins A and C. Try the flowers in a salad or cook the young shoots as a vegetable.

HERBS

Carrot Family (Apiaceae)

Cow-parsnip
Heracleum maximum

OTHER NAMES: Indian celery, Indian rhubarb; also known as *Heracleum lanatum*.
DESCRIPTION: Hairy perennial herb with hollow stems. **Height:** To 10' (3 m). **Flowers:** Small and white, shaped into an umbrella-like cluster. **Leaves:** Very large with palmate lobes.
HABITAT: Open meadows, moist slopes and forest edges.

When cow parsnip is mature it is hairy and strong-smelling. Some confuse it with several other similar-looking and **highly poisonous** plants. This common species is relished by a variety of wild and domestic animals, including elk, bear and mountain sheep.

Dogwood Family (Cornaceae)

Bunchberry
Cornus canadensis

OTHER NAME: Dwarf dogwood.
DESCRIPTION: Perennial herb with a somewhat woody base. **Height:** To 8" (20 cm).
Flowers: White, 4 petal-like bracts surround a cluster of tiny greenish flowers. **Leaves:** Whorled.
HABITAT: Coniferous and mixed wood forests; low to subalpine elevations.

The springtime carpet of white bunchberry flowers on the forest floor turn, in the summer, to bright red edible berries. These provide an important food source for many birds and mammals including the ruffed grouse and spruce grouse.

HERBS

Wintergreen Family (Pyrolaceae)

Single Delight
Moneses uniflora

OTHER NAMES: One-flowered wintergreen, wood nymph; also known as *Pyrola uniflora*.
DESCRIPTION: Evergreen perennial from rhizomes. **Height:** To 7" (17 cm).
Flowers: White, solitary and waxy.
Leaves: Basal, oval.
HABITAT: Moist coniferous forests.

Visit a forest from Alaska to Oregon and you will often be delighted to find this flower. The leaves, which are present all year, are similar to those of several other members of the wintergreen family, including prince's pine (p. 58) and green wintergreen (below).

Wintergreen Family (Pyrolaceae)

Green Wintergreen
Pyrola chlorantha

OTHER NAMES: Greenish-flowered wintergreen; also known as *P. virens*.
DESCRIPTION: Evergreen perennial from rhizomes. **Height:** To 10" (25 cm). **Flowers:** Greenish-white, curved style projects beyond petals, elongated cluster (raceme). **Leaves:** Basal, oval.
HABITAT: Coniferous and mixed forests.

Petite green wintergreen adds a delicate touch of color to the forest floor throughout much of the Pacific Northwest. Pink wintergreen (*Pyrola asarifolia*), named for its flowers, is a similar species.

HERBS

Wintergreen Family (Pyrolaceae)

One-sided Wintergreen
Orthilia secunda

OTHER NAMES: One-sided pyrola; also known as *Pyrola secunda*.
DESCRIPTION: Evergreen perennial from rhizomes. **Height:** To 8" (20 cm). **Flowers:** Light-green to white, elongated cluster. **Leaves:** Basal.
HABITAT: Coniferous and mixed forests.

It is easy to identify one-sided wintergreen by its distinctive flowers. The wintergreens were used for a wide variety of herbal remedies. The leaves contain acids believed to help skin problems. Nervous disorders such as epilepsy were thought to respond to a variety of species.

Wintergreen Family (Pyrolaceae)

Prince's Pine
Chimaphila umbellata

OTHER NAME: Pipsissewa.
DESCRIPTION: Small evergreen shrub from rhizomes. **Height:** To 12" (30 cm). **Flowers:** Pink, saucer-shaped.
Leaves: Whorled.
HABITAT: Well-drained coniferous forests.

Prince's pine was once used to add flavor to soft drinks and candy. Today this delicate inhabitant of dimly-lit coniferous forests is not as abundant as it once was and should be protected. Another similar species with alternate leaves, Menzie's pipsissewa (*Chimaphila menziesii*), is common on the coast where it reaches a maximum height of 6" (15 cm).

HERBS

Indian-pipe Family (Monotropaceae)

Indian-pipe
Monotropa uniflora

OTHER NAMES: Ice plant, corpse plant, ghost flower.
DESCRIPTION: Saprophyte. **Height:** To 10" (25 cm). **Flowers:** White, bell-like and waxy. **Leaves:** Scale-like.
HABITAT: Shady coniferous forests; low elevations.

Indian-pipe dates back to the Tertiary age. Found in dimly-lit sites, the entire plant is a "ghostly" white, hence a few of its common names. Lacking in chlorophyll, this species obtains its nutrients from the roots of nearby trees through a special relationship with fungi in the soil.

Indian-pipe Family (Monotropaceae)

Pinesap
Monotropa hypopitys

OTHER NAMES: False beech-drops, many-flowered Indian pipe; formerly *Hypopitys monotropa*.
DESCRIPTION: Saprophyte. **Height:** To 12" (30 cm). **Flowers:** Yellow to pink or red when fresh, urn-shaped. **Leaves:** Scale-like along the stem.
HABITAT: Coniferous forests; moderate elevations.

Pinesap, closely related to Indian-pipe (see above), is an intriguing species that lacks chlorophyll. This saprophyte's common name comes from its sap-like color and its home beneath conifer forests, particularly pine forests, from Alaska to California.

HERBS

Indian-pipe Family (Monotropaceae)

Pinedrops

Pterospora andromedea

OTHER NAME: Woodland pinedrops.
DESCRIPTION: Saprophyte that is sticky and hairy overall. **Height:** To 39" (1 m). **Flowers:** White, yellow or pink, urn-shaped, numerous on a single stalk. **Leaves:** Scale-like and lance-shaped.
HABITAT: Coniferous forests.

This beautiful saprophyte prefers to grow in deep humus soil under shaded hemlock and pine forests. There it produces an amazing number of tiny seeds. Each of these minute seeds possesses a tiny sail so it can ride the wind. Even so, only a few will survive.

Heath Family (Ericaceae)

Gnome-plant

Hemitomes congestum

OTHER NAME: Cone-plant.
DESCRIPTION: Saprophyte. **Height:** To 6" (15 cm). **Flowers:** Yellow-pink, bell-shaped, waxy. **Leaves:** Scale-like.
HABITAT: Damp coniferous forests; low to medium elevations

The gnome-plant grows only in isolated pockets from BC through to northern California. For those who venture into the forest, this

delicate species is a true gem.

HERBS

Primrose Family (Primulaceae)

Few-flowered Shootingstar

Dodecatheon pulchellum

OTHER NAMES: Pretty shootingstar; also known as *D. pauciflorum*.
DESCRIPTION: Perennial herb from roots that lack bulblets. **Height:** To 20" (50 cm).
Flowers: Magenta to lavender, yellow tube holds purple anthers, petals swept back.
Leaves: Basal, oblong.
HABITAT: Moist meadows, stream edges and similar areas; sea level to alpine.

The Latin pulchellum means beauty and this striking species shows its beauty from Alaska to Mexico. A similar species, broad-leaved shootingstar (*Dodecatheon hendersonii*) with a floral display of up to an amazing 22 blossoms, lives in drier areas of the Pacific Northwest.

Primrose Family (Primulaceae)

Broad-leaved Starflower

Trientalis latifolia

OTHER NAMES: Western starflower, Indian potato.
DESCRIPTION: Perennial from tubers. **Height:** To 12" (30 cm). **Flowers:** Pink to rose, somewhat star-shaped. **Leaves:** Alternate, large and broad.
HABITAT: Open forest, meadows.

The delicate flowers of the broad-leaved starflower carpet the edges of small openings in the forest floor. The round, white seed cases bear a remarkable resemblance to miniature soccer balls.

Buckbean Family (Menyanthaceae)

Buckbean
Menyanthes trifoliata

OTHER NAME: Bogbean.
DESCRIPTION: Aquatic or semi-aquatic perennial. **Height:** To 12" (30 cm). **Flowers:** White, occasionally pink, frilled. **Leaves:** Alternate, fleshy, with 3 leaflets.
HABITAT: Usually in shallow water.

Deer often browse the succulent buckbean. Its delicate, foul-smelling flowers attract a wide variety of insects including flies, beetles and bees, who certainly do not share the same olfactory values we do. Aboriginal peoples used this species to cure a wide variety of ailments.

Bindweed Family (Convolvulaceae)

Hedge Bindweed
Calystegia sepium

OTHER NAMES: Field bindweed, white morning glory, wild morning glory; *Convolvulus sepium*.
DESCRIPTION: Perennial herb from rhizomes that climbs or trails. **Height:** To 10' (3 m) long. **Flowers:** White to pink, funnel-shaped. **Leaves:** Alternate, arrow-shaped.
HABITAT: Open sites including disturbed areas.

Hedge bindweed was introduced from Europe. Now it is prolific across much of North America and is considered a weed. Its large, beautiful flowers display from May through September, but only when the sun shines. They close at night and on cloudy days. Field bindweed (*Convolvulus arvensis*), a similar-looking species, has smaller flowers that lack floral bracts.

HERBS

Phlox Family (Polemoniaceae)

Spreading Phlox
Phlox diffusa

OTHER NAMES: Mountain phlox; formerly known as *P. douglasii*.
DESCRIPTION: Perennial from a taproot. **Height:** To 4" (10 cm).
Flowers: Varies greatly from white to pink and purple or lavender, saucer-like with no stalk present. **Leaves:** Opposite, needle-like.
HABITAT: Open rocky areas; moderate to alpine elevations.

At higher elevations from southern BC to California beautiful mats of this showy wildflower hug the ground, adding a wonderful splash of color. The color variations within this species are truly remarkable. Pink clones often grow within a few footsteps of a white colony.

Phlox Family (Polemoniaceae)

Showy Jacob's Ladder
Polemonium pulcherrimum

OTHER NAMES: Sky pilot; also known as *P. delicatum*.
DESCRIPTION: Perennial herb from a taproot. **Height:** To 14" (35 cm).
Flowers: Blue with a yellow center, bell-shaped, clustered. **Leaves:** Basal, 11-25 leaflets.
HABITAT: Dry, rocky sites, open forests.

Showy Jacob's ladder's sweet smell attracts the insects necessary for pollination. Insects see color differently than we do because they rely primarily on ultraviolet light. The blue areas of this wildflower reflect ultraviolet light. Other areas of the flower, however, absorb ultraviolet light and produce a bull's eye effect for insects to "home in" on to find nectar.

HERBS

Waterleaf Family (Hydrophyllaceae)

Silky Phacelia
Phacelia sericea

OTHER NAMES: Sky-pilot, purple fringe, mountain phacelia, scorpionweed.
DESCRIPTION: Perennial with a woody stem base. Fine hairs cover much of the plant. **Height:** To 12" (30 cm).
Flowers: Deep purple with orange to yellow-tipped stamens, forms an elongated cluster. **Leaves:** Alternate, with deep divisions.
HABITAT: Dry rocky areas; moderate to alpine elevations.

This plant is aptly named; its fine hairs give it a distinctive silky look. Vivid purple blossoms show from June through August. Its scientific name sericea means "silky" while Phacelia is derived from the Greek word phakelos, which means "cluster" (referring to the flower cluster).

Borage Family (Boraginaceae)

Tall Bluebells
Mertensia paniculata

OTHER NAMES: Tall lungwort, bluebells.
DESCRIPTION: Perennial herb from rhizomes or woody base. **Height:** To 5' (1.5 m).
Flowers: Blue, bell-shaped, clustered. **Leaves:** Lance-shaped to oval or heart-shaped with conspicuous veins.
HABITAT: Moist meadows, open forest.

The delicate flowers of tall bluebells first appear pinkish before changing to their familiar blue. This species lives from low elevations through to alpine situations but it is more common at moderate elevations and higher from Alaska to central Oregon.

HERBS

Mint Family (Lamiaceae)

Self-heal
Prunella vulgaris

OTHER NAMES: Heal-all, woundwort.
DESCRIPTION: Perennial from rhizomes or stem base. **Height:** To 12" (30 cm), but normally smaller. **Flowers:** Purple to pink, lower lip is 3 lobed in a cluster at the tip of the plant. **Leaves:** Opposite.
HABITAT: Roadsides, forest edges and similar sites.

To appreciate the beauty of self-heal, take the time to look at the small flowers in detail. This species is now found on all continents. Aboriginal peoples used this plant as a cure for a wide variety of ailments including boils, bleeding, bruises and skin inflammations. Self-heal contains ursolic acid, which may fight tumors.

Mint Family (Lamiaceae)

Cooley's Hedge-nettle
Stachys cooleyae

OTHER NAMES: Great hedge nettle, purple hedge nettle.
DESCRIPTION: Perennial herb from rhizomes. **Height:** To 5' (1.5 m). **Flowers:** Reddish-purple, shaped in a long terminal cluster. **Leaves:** Opposite and heart-shaped to deltoid.
HABITAT: Shaded swamps and low-lying areas especially at low elevations.

Hummingbirds visit the colorful blooms of Cooley's hedge-nettle from June to August. The scientific name Stachys means "spike" in Greek. This refers to the arrangement of flowers on the upper portion of the plant. Look closely at the individual flowers of this species to see double anthers on each of the stamens.

65

HERBS

Mint Family (Lamiaceae)

Wild Bergamot
Monarda fistulosa

OTHER NAMES: Horse mint, purple bee's-balm; also known as *M. menthifolia*.
DESCRIPTION: Perennial herb from rhizomes. **Height:** To 39" (1 m). **Flowers:** Bright rose to purple, tubular and tightly crowded into a flat-topped cluster. **Leaves:** Opposite, toothed.
HABITAT: Arid areas, forest edge.

Aboriginal peoples used aromatic wild bergamot as a perfume. They also burned the plants on hot rocks in sweat baths as incense and as a smudge for repelling insects. Therapeutic uses included healing wounds, relieving painful swollen joints and reducing fevers.

Figwort Family (Scrophulariaceae)

Common Red Paintbrush
Castilleja miniata

OTHER NAMES: Western Indian paintbrush, painted cup.
DESCRIPTION: Perennial from a woody base. **Height:** To 32" (80 cm). **Flowers:** Pointed red bracts hide the greenish flowers. **Leaves:** Linear to lanceolate.
HABITAT: Open forests, meadows; at all elevations.

Growing singly or together in great profusion, this species, the most common of many Pacific Northwest paintbrushes, produces a memorable palette of vivid red to scarlet. Its leaves photosynthesize like most plants, however, it is also semi-parasitic on the roots of other plants.

HERBS

Figwort Family (Scrophulariaceae)

Small-flowered Blue-eyed Mary

Collinsia parviflora

OTHER NAME: Blue-eyed Mary.
DESCRIPTION: Annual herb.
Height: To 16" (40 cm) but normally much smaller. **Flowers:** Blue with a little white, two lips are present, to 3/8" (8 mm) long. **Leaves:** Opposite.
HABITAT: Moist open areas; low to middle elevations and occasionally higher.

Ranging from Alaska to California, this species' small flowers carpet rocky outcroppings with early blossoms, one of the first signs of spring. This wildflower sometimes accompanies sea blush (p. 66). Large-flowered blue-eyed Mary (*Collinsia grandiflora*) is a similar species with longer flowers 3/8-5/8" (8-17 mm) and more white on the upper lip.

Figwort Family (Scrophulariaceae)

Yellow Monkey-flower

Mimulus guttatus

OTHER NAME: Common monkey-flower.
DESCRIPTION: Perennial or annual.
Height: To 32" (80 cm). **Flowers:** Bright yellow, trumpet-shaped. **Leaves:** Paired, oval, toothed.
HABITAT: Moist areas, rock outcrops; low to subalpine elevations.

This vibrant species has an interesting way to transfer pollen from one flower to another. When an insect, covered with pollen from one flower, comes to dine on the nectar of another, it touches two round parts of the stigma, which immediately fold together. This transfers pollen collected from the first flower onto the stigma of the second for fertilization.

HERBS

Figwort Family (Scrophulariaceae)

Slender Blue Penstemon
Penstemon procerus

OTHER NAMES: Small-flowered penstemon, tall penstemon, blue beard-tongue.
DESCRIPTION: Perennial herb from woody roots. **Height:** To 16" (40 cm). **Flowers:** Blue-purple, occasionally cream-colored, tubular, arranged in whorls around the stem. **Leaves:** Basal, smooth edged.
HABITAT: Dry sandy areas.

Slender blue penstemon, the most common of many types of penstemon in the Pacific Northwest, is a vibrant species with a long list of names. Its common name, beard-tongue, originates from the hairy throat and lower lip of its flowers.

Broomrape Family (Orobanchaceae)

Vancouver Groundcone
Boschniakia hookeri

OTHER NAMES: Ground-cone, poque.
DESCRIPTION: Parasitic herb. **Height:** To 5" (12 cm). **Flowers:** Color varies from yellow to purple. **Leaves:** Scale-like and numerous forming a spike-like shape similar to a conifer's cone.
HABITAT: Forest edge along the coast.

Vancouver groundcone, which looks like a fir cone stuck upright in the ground, is a root parasite of several plants, especially salal (p. 24). A single plant produces over 300,000 seeds but few grow successfully. This species ranges from southern BC to northern California.

HERBS

Bladderwort Family (Lentibulariaceae)

Common Butterwort
Pinguicula vulgaris

OTHER NAMES: Butterwort; *Utricularia vulgaris*.
DESCRIPTION: Perennial herb with fibrous roots. **Height:** To 6" (15 cm). **Flowers:** Purple, petals funnel-shaped. **Leaves:** Basal, lance-shaped, fleshy.
HABITAT: Bogs, fens and similar wet areas.

This insectivorous plant, which lives in nitrogen-poor areas, uses a sticky covering on its upper leaf surface to trap insects. Digestive enzymes absorb nutrients, including nitrogen, from the insects. This remarkable plant also photosynthesizes as most flowering plants do.

Plantain Family (Plantaginaceae)

Seaside Plantain
Plantago maritima

OTHER NAMES: Sea plantain, goose-tongue.
DESCRIPTION: Perennial from a taproot. **Height:** To 10" (25 cm). **Flowers:** Green, shaped into several dense spikes. **Leaves:** Basal, fleshy and linear.
HABITAT: Ocean beaches.

Seaside plantain can flourish in amazingly small amounts of soil collected in crevices of large seashore boulders. Its greenish blossoms largely go unnoticed. This widespread species also grows in Eurasia, Patagonia and the Galapagos Islands.

HERBS

Valerian Family (Valerianaceae)

Sea Blush
Plectritis congesta

OTHER NAMES: Rosy plectritis, shortspur seablush.
DESCRIPTION: Annual. **Height:** To 24" (60 cm). **Flowers:** Pink or white, clustered in terminal flower heads. **Leaves:** Opposite, oblong.
HABITAT: Moist meadows and grassy bluffs.

From late February to May, sea blush lays a beautiful pink floral carpet next to the ocean from southern BC to southern California. It's scientific name, congesta means congested or crowded.

Harebell Family (Campanulaceae)

Common Harebell
Campanula rotundifolia

OTHER NAMES: Bluebell, bluebells-of-Scotland.
DESCRIPTION: Perennial herb from rhizomes or taproot. **Height:** To 32" (80 cm). **Flowers:** Blue, bell-shaped. **Leaves:** Basal, oval or heart-shaped.
HABITAT: Grassy areas, open woods; sea level to subalpine elevations.

A long, slender stalk supports the delicate flowers of common harebell even in the strongest of winds. This species is found from Alaska to California and in Scotland and Switzerland. On rare occasions common harebell has white flowers.

HERBS

Aster Family (Asteraceae)

Pale Agoseris
Agoseris glauca

OTHER NAMES: False dandelion, pale mountain dandelion, short-beaked agoseris.
DESCRIPTION: Perennial herb.
Height: To 28" (70 cm). **Flowers:** Yellow, solitary with only ray florets present. **Leaves:** Basal, rosette, lanceolate.
HABITAT: Open coniferous forest.

Pale agoseris ranges from Alaska through to northern California. Except for its distinctive leaves that lack pronounced lobes, it looks similar to common dandelion. Both species have milky sap.

Aster Family (Asteraceae)

Yellow Salsify
Tragopogon dubius

OTHER NAME: Goat's-beard.
DESCRIPTION: Biennial herb from a taproot. **Height:** To 39" (1 m).
Flowers: Pale yellow, ray florets only, solitary. **Leaves:** Grass-like.
HABITAT: Open wayside.

Yellow salsify is easy to miss because it is matutinal. (It opens its flowers only until noon on sunny days.) The seed head resembles that of the common dandelion. The roots make a pleasant addition to a fresh salad. They can also be boiled, roasted or fried.

HERBS

Aster Family (Asteraceae)

Yarrow
Achillea millefolium

OTHER NAMES: Common yarrow, milfoil.
DESCRIPTION: Perennial herb from rhizomes. **Height:** To 39" (1 m). **Flowers:** White, occasionally pinkish, small flowers clustered into a flat top. **Leaves:** Pinnate, fern-like.
HABITAT: Open, well-drained sites, roadsides.

Yarrow produces over one hundred ingredients proven effective in treating a wide variety of ailments. This plant affects the cardio-vascular system (lowering blood pressure and slowing the heartbeat). As a tea, it raises the body temperature to induce sweating. Aboriginal peoples used yarrow to relieve stomach disorders, headaches, sore eyes, bronchitis, measles, diarrhea, coughs and colds.

Aster Family (Asteraceae)

Pearly Everlasting
Anaphalis margaritacea

DESCRIPTION: Perennial from rhizomes. **Height:** To 24" (60 cm). **Flowers:** Yellow center surrounded by whitish bracts, form a flat-topped cluster. **Leaves:** Narrow and alternate.
HABITAT: Dry, open sites.

Pearly everlasting grows from sea level to mountain heights. Aboriginal peoples used it to make poultices for sores, bruises and swellings. Its leaves have been used as a tobacco. As a medicinal tea it also treated colds, throat infections and upset stomachs. Now this native of North America is used in dried floral arrangements.

HERBS

Aster Family (Asteraceae)

Edible Thistle

Cirsium edule

OTHER NAMES: Edible Indian thistle, Indian thistle.
DESCRIPTION: Perennial or biennial from a taproot. **Height:** To 79" (2 m). **Flowers:** Purple head, dense, woolly hairs present. **Leaves:** Alternate, elongated with irregular teeth (greater than half the width), spines present on outer bracts.
HABITAT: Moist meadows and clearings.

Edible thistle is more common at higher elevations, where it blooms from April through September. It obtained its common name because aboriginal peoples and settlers peeled and ate the young stems. Take the time to see its delicate blossom pattern and the dense, wooly hairs beneath.

Aster Family (Asteraceae)

Bull Thistle

Cirsium vulgare

OTHER NAMES: Common thistle, spear thistle, Scotch thistle.
DESCRIPTION: Biennial from a taproot. **Height:** To 5' (1.5 m). **Flowers:** Rose-purple, large heads.
Leaves: Alternate, deeply cleft.
HABITAT: Waste areas, roadsides.

Bull thistle is a spiny wonder indeed. Its leaves are armed with prickles on both the upper surface and along the edge. Rigid, yellow-tipped spines grace the flower bracts as well as the stem. People consider this European species a weed but its flowers are a favorite of a wide variety of butterflies.

HERBS

Aster Family (Asteraceae)

Oxeye Daisy
Leucanthemum vulgare

OTHER NAMES: Manguerite; formerly *Chrysanthemum leucanthemum*.
DESCRIPTION: Perennial herb from rhizomes. **Height:** To 32" (80 cm). **Flowers:** White rays surround a yellow center. **Leaves:** Alternate, basal, oblong to spatulate.
HABITAT: Open meadows, roadsides and disturbed areas.

The oxeye daisy, introduced from Europe, now inhabits much of North America. This is a common wayside species that smells like sage. Scentless chamomile (*Matricaria perforata*) is a similar species that does not emit a fragrance as its common name suggests. Its leaves are divided into many thread-like segments.

Aster Family (Asteraceae)

Brown-eyed Susan
Gaillardia aristata

OTHER NAME: Wild gaillardia.
DESCRIPTION: Perennial from a taproot. **Height:** To 28" (70 cm). **Flowers:** Yellow ray flowers, brownish-purple disc flowers, woolly, daisy-shape. **Leaves:** Basal, lanceolate.
HABITAT: Arid areas, grasslands, open coniferous forest.

This wildflower's spectacular flower heads add a welcome splash of color to dry areas. Aboriginal peoples employed this common species for a wide variety of uses including eye drops, dandruff shampoo and a cure for venereal disease. Today it is an attractive addition to native gardens.

HERBS

Aster Family (Asteraceae)

Entire-leaved Gumweed

Grindelia integrifolia

OTHER NAMES: Gum weed, resinweed.
DESCRIPTION: Perennial herb from a taproot base. **Height:** To 32" (80 cm).
Flowers: Yellow, up to 35 on a single plant. **Leaves:** Alternate, large, rigid and lance-shaped.
HABITAT: Ocean beaches, open meadows.

This common wildflower grows on rocky shores and beaches of maritime habitats as well as in moist areas elsewhere. It gets its name from a white, gum-like sticky secretion produced by the bracts that surround each immature flower head. Its long-lasting blossoms attract a wide variety of insects including several butterflies and beetles.

Aster Family (Asteraceae)

Orange Hawkweed

Hieracium aurantiacum

OTHER NAME: Devil's paintbrush.
DESCRIPTION: Perennial herb from stolons and rhizomes.
Height: To 16" (40 cm). **Flowers:** Red-orange, ray flowers only.
Leaves: Basal, rosette.
HABITAT: Roadsides and disturbed areas.

Orange hawkweed, with a coloration that is both striking and distinctive, is an introduced species from Europe and is classified as an aggressive weed. It is expanding its range along man's highway corridors. It is densely covered with blackish hairs and a milky fluid is released when its stem is broken.

HERBS

Aster Family (Asteraceae)

Palmate Coltsfoot
Petasites palmatus

OTHER NAME: Palm-leaved coltsfoot.
DESCRIPTION: Perennial herb from rhizomes. **Height:** To 20" (50 cm).
Flowers: Cream-colored, clustered.
Leaves: Basal, deeply divided with 4-7 lobes.
HABITAT: Wet meadows, moist roadsides.

The early, delicate flowers of palmate coltsfoot announce spring as they begin to bloom before the leaves are present. Male and female flowers usually exist on separate heads. Aboriginal peoples used the leaves to cover berries in steam cooking pits.

Aster Family (Asteraceae)

Douglas' Aster
Aster subspicatus

OTHER NAME: Also known as *A. douglasii*.
DESCRIPTION: Perennial herb from rhizomes or stem base with a hairy upper stem. **Height:** To 32" (80 cm). **Flowers:** Purple to bluish rays with a yellow central disc, several to many per plant.
Leaves: Lance-shaped to oblong.
HABITAT: Seashore, open forest and near streams; low to moderate elevations.

This beautiful species, common along the coast from Alaska to northern California, attracts a wide assortment of butterflies. Several additional asters also live throughout the Pacific Northwest. Leafy aster (*Aster foliaceus*) is a similar species with wider leaves and ray flowers with white edges at the base.

Additional Reading

Clark, Lewis J. 1998. (third edition). *Wild Flowers of the Pacific Northwest*. Harbour Publishing, Madeira Park, British Columbia

Horn, E.L. 1994. *Coastal Wildflowers of British Columbia and the Pacific Northwest*. Whitecap Books, Vancouver, British Columbia

Kershaw, Linda, A. MacKinnon and J. Pojar. 1998. *Plants of the Rocky Mountains*. Lone Pine Publishing, Edmonton, Alberta

Lyons, C.P. 1997. *Wildflowers of Washington*. Lone Pine Publishing, Edmonton, Alberta

MacKinnon, Andy, J. Pojar and R. Coupe. 1999. (second edition). *Plants of Northern British Columbia*. Lone Pine Publishing, Edmonton, Alberta

Pojar, Jim and A. MacKinnon. 1994. *Plants of Coastal British Columbia including Washington, Oregon and Alaska*. Lone Pine Publishing, Edmonton, Alberta

Qiaan, Hong and K. Klinka. 1998. *Plants of British Columbia*. UBC Press, Vancouver, British Columbia

Strickler, Dee. 1993. *Wayside Wildflowers of the Pacific Northwest: Showy Wildflowers along the Roads and Highways, Trails and Byways of the Pacific Northwest*. The Flower Press, Columbia Falls, Montana

Turner, Nancy J. 1995. *Food Plants of Coastal First Peoples*. Royal British Columbia Museum Handbook, UBC Press, Vancouver, British Columbia

Acknowledgments

I would like to thank several people who assisted with this project.

Audrey Owen for her careful and passionate editing.

Jim Salt (Victoria, BC) generously aided me in locating several wildflower species for photography.

The staff at various provincial and state parks throughout British Columbia, Washington and Oregon, especially at Manning Provincial Park, BC, who helped locate species and provide site information.

Mike Hawkes (University of British Columbia, Vancouver, BC) was kind enough to confirm the identification of several species of wildflowers.

CHECKLIST

Wildflower Checklist

FLOWERING TREES AND SHRUBS

Barberry Family (Berberidaceae)
❑ Tall Oregon-grape *Mahonia aquifolium* ....

Rose Family (Rosaceae)
❑ Pacific Crab Apple *Malus fusca* ....
❑ Ocean Spray *Holodiscus discolor* ....
❑ Saskatoon *Amelanchier alnifolia* ....
❑ Indian Plum *Oemlaria cerasiformis* ....
❑ Pacific Ninebark *Physocarpus capitatus* ....
❑ Nootka Rose *Rosa nutkana*..
❑ Clustered Wild Rose *Rosa pisocarpa* ....
❑ Baldhip Rose *Rosa gymnocarpa*..
❑ Salmonberry *Rubus spectabilis* ....
❑ Thimbleberry *Rubus parviflorus* ....
❑ Himalayan Blackberry *Rubus discolor* ....
❑ Trailing Blackberry *Rubus ursinus* ....
❑ Pink Spiraea *Spiraea douglasii* ....

Pea Family (Fabaceae)
❑ Scotch Broom *Cytisus scoparius* ....

Dogwood Family (Cornaceae)
❑ Pacific Dogwood *Cornus nuttallii* ....

Heath Family (Ericaceae)
❑ Arbutus *Arbutus menziesii* ....
❑ Salal *Gaultheria shallon* ....
❑ Black Huckleberry *Vaccinium membranaceum* ....
❑ Red huckleberry *Vaccinium parvifolium* ....
❑ White Rhododendron *Rhododendron albiflorum* ....
❑ Pacific Rhododendron *Rhododendron macrophyllum* ....
❑ Bog-laurel *Kalmia microphylla* ....
❑ Common Bearberry *Arctostaphylos uva-ursi* ....

Honeysuckle Family (Caprifoliaceae)
❑ Twinflower *Linnaea borealis* ....
❑ Western Trumpet Honeysuckle *Lonicera ciliosa* ....
❑ Bracted Honeysuckle *Lonicera involucrata* ....
❑ Red Elderberry *Sambucus racemosa* ....

CHECKLIST

FLOWERING HERBS & NON-WOODY PLANTS

Cattail Family (Typhaceae)
❑ Common Cattail *Typha latifolia* ....
Sedge Family (Cyperaceae)
❑ Many-spiked Cottongrass *Eriophorum angustifolium* ....
Arum Family (Araceae)
❑ Skunk Cabbage *Lysichiton americanus* ....
Lily Family (Liliaceae)
❑ False Solomon's Seal *Maianthemum racemosum* ....
❑ Western Trillium *Trillium ovatum* ....
❑ False Lily-of-the-valley *Maianthemum dilatatum* ....
❑ Queen's Cup *Clintonia uniflora* ....
❑ White Fawn Lily *Erythronium oregonum* ....
❑ Nodding Onion *Allium cernuum* ....
❑ Fool's Onion *Triteleia hyacinthina* ....
❑ Meadow Death-camas *Zygadenus venenosus* ....
❑ Common Camas *Camassia quamash* ....
❑ Chocolate Lily *Fritillaria lanceolata* ....
❑ Tiger Lily *Lilium columbianum* ....
❑ Beargrass *Xerophyllum tenax* ....
Iris Family (Iridaceae)
❑ Yellow-flag *Iris pseudacorus* ....
Orchid Family (Orchidaceae)
❑ Fairyslipper *Calypso bulbosa* ....
❑ Mountain Ladyslipper *Cypripedium montanum* ....
❑ Spotted Coralroot *Corallorhiza maculata* ....
❑ Striped Coralroot *Corallorhiza striata* ....
❑ Pale Coralroot *Corallorhiza trifida* ....
Nettle Family (Urticaceae)
❑ Stinging Nettle *Urtica dioica* ....
Mistletoe Family (Loranthaceae)
❑ American Dwarf Mistletoe *Arceuthobium americanum* ....
Buckwheat Family (Polygonaceae)
❑ Water Smartweed *Polygonum amphibium* ....
Goosefoot Family (Chenopodiaceae)
❑ Strawberry Blight *Chenopodium capitatum* ....
Water-lily Family (Nymphaeaceae)
❑ Yellow Pond-lily *Nuphar polysepalum* ....

CHECKLIST

Heath Family (Ericaceae)
❏ Gnome-plant *Hemitomes congestum* ....

Primrose Family (Primulaceae)
❏ Few-flowered Shootingstar *Dodecatheon pulchellum* ....
❏ Broad-leaved Shootingstar *Dodecatheon hendersonii* ....
❏ Broad-leaved Starflower *Trientalis latifolia* ....

Buckbean Family (Menyanthaceae)
❏ Buckbean *Menyanthes trifoliata* ....

Bindweed Family (Convolvulaceae)
❏ Hedge Bindweed *Calystegia sepium* ....
❏ Field Bindweed *Convolvulus arvensis* ....

Phlox Family (Polemoniaceae)
❏ Spreading Phlox *Phlox diffusa* ....
❏ Showy Jacob's Ladder *Polemonium pulcherrimum* ....

Waterleaf Family (Hydrophyllaceae)
❏ Silky Phacelia *Phacelia sericea* ....

Borage Family (Boraginaceae)
❏ Tall Bluebells *Mertensia paniculata* ....

Mint Family (Lamiaceae)
❏ Self-heal *Prunella vulgaris* ....
❏ Cooley's Hedge-nettle *Stachys cooleyae* ....
❏ Wild Bergamot *Monarda fistulosa* ....

Figwort Family (Scrophulariaceae)
❏ Common Red Paintbrush *Castilleja miniata* ....
❏ Small-flowered Blue-eyed Mary *Collinsia parviflora* ....
❏ Large-flowered Blue-eyed Mary *Collinsia grandiflora* ....
❏ Yellow Monkey-flower *Mimulus guttatus* ....
❏ Slender Blue Penstemon *Penstemon procerus* ....

Broomrape Family (Orobanchaceae)
❏ Vancouver Groundcone *Boschniakia hookeri* ....

Bladderwort Family (Lentibulariaceae)
❏ Common Butterwort *Pinguicula vulgaris* ....

Plantain Family (Plantaginaceae)
❏ Seaside Plantain *Plantago maritima* ....

Valerian Family (Valerianaceae)
❏ Sea Blush *Plectritis congesta* ....

Harebell Family (Campanulaceae)
❏ Common Harebell *Campanula rotundifolia* ....

CHECKLIST

Aster Family (Asteraceae)

❑ Pale Agoseris *Agoseris glauca* ....
❑ Yellow Salsify *Tragopogon dubius* ....
❑ Yarrow *Achillea millefolium* ....
❑ Pearly Everlasting *Anaphalis margaritacea* ....
❑ Edible Thistle *Cirsium edule* ....
❑ Bull Thistle *Cirsium vulgare* ....
❑ Oxeye Daisy *Leucanthemum vulgare* ....
❑ Brown-eyed Susan *Gaillardia aristata* ....
❑ Entire-leaved Gumweed *Grindelia integrifolia* ....
❑ Orange Hawkweed *Hieracium aurantiacum* ....
❑ Palmate Coltsfoot *Petasites palmatus* ....
❑ Douglas' Aster *Aster subspicatus* ....
❑ Leafy Aster *Aster foliaceus* ....

Notes:

....
....
....
....
....
....
....
....
....

Index

A

Achillea millefolium, 72
Achlys triphylla, 45
Actaea rubra, 43
Agoseris glauca, 71
agoseris, short-beaked, 71
Allium cernuum, 33
alum root, 48
alumroot, small-flowered, 48
Amelanchier alnifolia, 18
Anaphalis margaritacea, 72
Anemone occidentalis, 42
anemone, western, 42
ant seed dispersal, 31, 45
Aquilegia
    flavescens, 44
    formosa, 44
Arbutus menziesii, 24
arbutus, 24
Arceuthobium americanum, 40
Arctostaphylos uva-ursi, 27
arum, yellow, 30
Aruncus
    dioicus, 50
    sylvester, 50
Aster
    douglasii, 76
    foliaceus, 76
    subspicatus, 76
aster,
    Douglas', 76
    leafy, 76
    big-leaved, 51
    large-leaved, 51
    purple, 51
avens, three-flowered, 51
azalea, Cascades, 25

B

baneberry, 43
    red, 43
bare-stemmed mitrewort, 47
bearberry, common, 27
beard-tongue, blue, 68
beargrass, 36
beech-drops, false, 59
Berberis aquifolium, 17
bergamot, wild, 66
bilberry, mountain, 26
bindweed,
    field, 62
    hedge, 62
bishop's cap, 47
blackberry,
    Himalayan, 21
    Pacific, 22
    trailing, 22
    trailing wild, 22
bleeding heart, Pacific, 45
blue-bead, 32
bluebell, 70
bluebells, 64
    tall, 64
bluebells-of-Scotland, 70
blueberry, black, 26
blue-eyed Mary, 67
    large-flowered, 67
    small-flowered, 67
bogbean, 62
bog-laurel, 26
    small, 26
    western, 26
Boschniakia hookeri, 68
Brodiaea hyacinthina, 34
broom, 23
    Scotch, 23

83

brown-eyed Susan, 74
buckbean, 62
bunchberry, 56
buttercup,
creeping, 43
meadow, 43
tall, 43
butterwort, 69
common, 69

C

Caltha leptosepala, 42
Calypso bulbosa, 37
Calystegia sepium, 62
camas,
common, 34
death, 34
poison, 34
Camassia quamash, 34
Campanula rotundifolia, 70
Castilleja miniata, 66
cattail, 29
broad-leaved, 29
common, 29
chalice flower, 42
chamomile, scentless, 74
Chenopodium capitatum, 41
Chimaphila menziesii, 58
Chimaphila umbellata, 58
Chrysanthemum leucanthemum, 74
Cirsium
edule, 73
vulgare, 73
clematis
blue, 44
Clematis
occidentalis, 44
verticillaris, 44
Clintonia uniflora, 32
clintonia, one-flowered, 32
clover,
Alsike, 53
peavine, 53
purple, 53
red, 53

white, 53
Collinsia
grandiflora, 67
parviflora, 67
coltsfoot,
palmate, 76
palm-leaved, 76
columbine,
red, 44
Sitka, 44
western, 44
yellow, 44
cone-plant, 60
Convolvulus
arvensis, 62
sepium, 62
Corallorhiza
maculata, 38
striata, 38
trifida, 39
coralroot,
northern, 39
pale, 39
spotted, 38
striped, 38
striped, 38
yellow, 39
corn-lily, 32
Cornus
canadensis, 56
nuttallii, 23
corpse plant, 59
cottongrass,
many-spiked, 30
narrow-leaved, 30
tall, 30
cowgrass, 53
cow-lily, 41
cow-parsnip, 56
crab apple,
Pacific, 17
western, 17
crabapple, wild, 17
cranesbill, sticky purple, 54

Cypripedium montanum, 37
Cytisus scoparius, 23
D
daisy, oxeye, 74
dandelion,
    false, 71
    pale mountain, 71
death-camas, meadow, 34
deerberry, 32
deerfoot, 45
dewberry, 22
Dicentra formosa, 45
Dodecatheon
    hendersonii, 61
    pauciflorum, 61
    pulchellum, 61
dogwood,
dwarf, 56
    flowering, 23
dogwood,
    Pacific, 23
    western, 23
Douglas spiraea, 22
Drosera rotundifolia, 46
E
elderberry,
    black, 29
    red, 29
elkslip, 42
Epilobium angustifolium, 55
Eriophorum
    angustifolium, 30
    polystachion, 30
Erythronium oregonum, 33
everlasting, pearly, 72
F
fairyslipper, 37
false spikenard, 31
fireweed, 55
flax,
    western blue, 55
    wild blue, 55
foamflower, 49
Fragaria

chiloensis, 50
glauca, 50
vesca, 50
virginiana, 50
fringecup, 48
    tall, 48
Fritillaria lanceolata, 35
G
Gaillardia aristata, 74
gaillardia, wild, 74
Gaultheria shallon, 24
geraniium, Robert, 54
Geranium
    robertianum, 54
    viscosissimum, 54
geranium,
    sticky purple, 54
    sticky, 54
    stinky, 54
Geum
    macrophyllum, 51
    triflorum, 51
ghost flower, 59
gnome-plant, 60
goat's beard, 50
goatsbeard, 50
goat's-beard, 71
goose-tongue, 69
grass-of-parnassus, fringed, 49
great willowherb, 55
Grindelia integrifolia, 75
ground-cone, 68
    Vancouver, 68
gum weed, 75
gumweed, entire-leaved, 75
H
hardhack, 22
harebell, common, 70
hawkweed, orange, 75
heal-all, 65
hedge nettle,
    great, 65
    purple, 65
hedge-nettle, Cooley's, 65

Hemitomes congestum, 60
Heracleum
    lanatum, 56
    maximum, 56
herb Robert, 54
Heuchera micrantha, 48
Hieracium aurantiacum, 75
Holodiscus discolor, 18
honeysuckle,
    bearberry, 28
    bracted, 28
    fly, 28
    orange, 28
    western trumpet, 28
horse mint, 66
huckleberry,
    black, 26
    mountain, 26
    red, 26
Hypopitys monotropa, 59

I
ice plant, 59
Indian celery, 56
Indian pipe, many-flowered, 59
Indian plant, 41
Indian plum, 19
Indian rhubarb, 56
Indian rice, 35
Indian spinach, 39
Indian-pipe, 59
Iris pseudacorus, 36
ironwood, 18

J
Jacob's ladder, showy, 63
juneberry, 18

K
Kalmia
    microphylla, 26
    polifolia, 26
kinnikinnick, 27

L
lace flower, 49
lady's slipper, white, 37
ladyslipper,

false, 37
    mountain, 37
ladysthumb, 40
large-leaved lupine, 53
Lathyrus
    japonicus, 52
    maritimus, 52
laurel,
    mountain, 26
    swamp, 26
Leucanthemum vulgare, 74
light,
    effects on flowers, 71
    ultraviolet, 63
Lilium columbianum, 35
lily,
    bead, 32
    checker, 35
    chocolate, 35
    Columbia, 35
    Easter, 33
    Oregon, 35
    skunk, 35
    tiger, 35
    white fawn, 33
    white trout, 33
lily-of-the-valley,
    false, 32
    two-leaved false, 32
Linnaea borealis, 27
linnaea, 27
Linum
    lewisii, 55
    perenne, 55
Lonicera
    ciliosa, 28
    involucrata, 28
lungwort, tall, , 64
lupine,
    arctic, 53
    subalpine broad-leaved, 53
Lupinus
    arcticus, 53
    latifolius, 53

polyphyllus, 53
Lysichiton
    americanus, 30
    americanum, 30

M
madder-stripes, 38
madrone, 24
    Pacific, 24
Mahonia aquifolium, 17
mahonia, tall, 17
Maianthemum
    dilatatum, 32
    racemosum, 31
Malus fusca, 17
manguerite, 74
marsh-marigold,
    alpine white, 42
    mountain, 42
Matricaria perforata, 74
may-leaf, 45
Menyanthes trifoliata, 62
Mertensia paniculata, 64
milfoil, 72
Mimulus guttatus, 67
mission bell, 35
mistletoe,
    American dwarf, 40
    Christmas, 40
    dwarf, 40
Mitella nuda, 47
mitrewort,
    common, 47
    false, 49
moccasin flower, 37
Monarda
    fistulosa, 66
    menthifolia, 66
Moneses uniflora, 57
monkey-flower,
    common, 67
    yellow, 67
Monotropa
    hypopitys, 59
    uniflora, 59

moptop, 42
morning glory,
    white, 62
    wild, 62
mountain phacelia, 64

N
nettle, stinging, 39
nine bark, 19
ninebark, Pacific, 19
northwest nettle, 39
Nuphar
    luteum, 41
    polysepalum, 41
Nymphaea odorata, 41

O
ocean spray, 18
Oemlaria cerasiformis, 19
old man's whiskers, 51
onion,
    fool's, 34
    nodding, 33
orchid,
    calypso, 37
    pink slipper, 37
Oregon-grape, tall, 17
Orthilia secunda, 58
Osmaronia cerasiformis, 19
osoberry, 19

P
paintbrush,
    common red, 66
    devil's, 75
    western Indian, 66
painted cup, 66
pale agoseris, 71
Parnassia fimbriata, 49
pasque flower, western, 42
pea, beach, 52
Penstemon procerus, 68
penstemon,
    slender blue, 68
    small-flowered, 68
    tall, 68
Petasites palmatus, 76

Phacelia sericea, 64
Phlox
    diffusa, 63
    douglasii, 63
phlox,
    mountain, 63
    spreading, 63
Phoradendron flavescens, 40
Physocarpus capitatus, 19
pinedrops, 60
    woodland, 60
pinesap, 59
Pinguicula vulgaris, 69
pipsissewa, 58
    Menzie's, 58
Plantago maritima, 69
plantain,
    sea, 69
    seaside, 69
Plectritis congesta, 70
plectritis, rosy, 70
plum, Indian, 19
Polemonium
    delicatum, 63
    pulcherrimum, 63
Polygonum amphibium, 40
pond-lily, yellow, 41
poque, 68
potato, Indian, 61
prairie smoke, 51
prince's pine, 58
Prunella vulgaris, 65
Pterospora andromedea, 60
purple bee's-balm, 66
purple fringe, 64
Pyrola
    asarifolia, 57
    chlorantha, 57
    secunda, 58
    uniflora, 57
    virens, 57
pyrola, one-sided, 58
Pyrus fusca, 17

Q
queen's cup, 32
R
Ranunculus
    acris, 43
    repens, 43
resinweed, 75
Rhododendron
    albiflorum, 25
    macrophyllum, 25
rhododendron,
    California, 25
    native, 25
    Pacific, 25
    pink, 25
    red, 25
    white, 25
    white-flowered, 25
rice-root, 35
Rosa
    gymnocarpa, 20
    nutkana, 20
    pisocarpa, 20
rose,
    baldhip, 20
    clustered wild, 20
    common wild, 20
    Nootka, 20
roseroot, 47
Rubus
    discolor, 21
    parviflorus, 21
    procerus, 21
    spectabilis, 20
    ursinus, 22
S
salal, 24, 68
salmonberry, 20
salsify, yellow, 71
Sambucus
    racemosa, 29
    racemosa var. *melanocarpa*, 29
    racemosa var. *pubens*, 29
saskatoon, 18

scorpionweed, 64
sea blush, 70
seablush, shortspur, 70
Sedum
    integrifolium, 47
    lanceolatum, 46
    oreganum, 46
    rosea, 47
    spathulifolium, 46
self-heal, 65
serviceberry, 18
shadbush, 18
shootingstar,
    broad-leaved, 61
    few-flowered, 61
    pretty, 61
silky phacelia, 64
single delight, 57
skunk cabbage, 30
    western, 30
sky pilot, 63, 64
slipper, Venus', 37
smartweed, water, 40
Smilacina racemosa, 31
Solomon's seal,
    false, 31
    two-leaved, 32
spaghetti flower, 50
spatterdock, 41
Spiraea
    douglasii, 22
    menziesii, 22
spiraea, pink, 22
Stachys cooleyae, 65
starflower,
    broad-leaved, 61
    western, 61
steeplebush, 22
stinky bob, 54
stonecrop,
    broadleaf, 46
    broad-leaved, 46
    lance-leaved, 46
    Oregon, 46

strawberry blight, 41
strawberry,
    coastal, 50
    Virginia, 50
    wild, 50
    wood, 50
sundew, round-leaved, 46
swamp lantern, 30
sweet-after-death, 45
T
Tellima grandiflora, 48
thimbleberry, 21
thistle,
    bull, 73
    common, 73
    edible, 73
    edible Indian, 73
    Indian, 73
    Scotch, 73
    spear, 73
Tiarella
    laciniata, 49
    trifoliata, 49
    unifoliata, 49
tow-headed baby, 42
Tragopogon dubius, 71
Trientalis latifolia, 61
Trifolium
    hybridum, 53
    pratense, 53
    repens, 53
Trillium ovatum, 31
trillium, western, 31
*Triteleia hyacinthin*a, 34
twinberry, black, 28
twinflower, 27
Typha latifolia, 29
U
Urtica dioica, 39
Utricularia vulgaris, 69
V
Vaccinium
    membranaceum, 26
    parvifolium, 26

89

vanilla Leaf, 45
vetch,
  bird, 52
  cow, 52
  tufted, 52
  wooly, 52
Vicia
  cracca, 52
  villosa, 52
virgin's bower, blue, 44

W
wake robin, 31
water lily, yellow, 41
waterlily, fragrant, 41
western bleeding heart, 45
white triteleia, 34
willow-herb, 55
wintergreen,
  green, 57
  greenish-flowered, 57
  one-flowered, 57
  one-sided, 58
  pink, 57
wood nymph, 57
woundwort, 65

X
Xerophyllum tenax, 36

Y
yarrow, 72
  common, 72
yellow flag, 36
yellow-flag, 36

Z
Zerophyllum, 36
Zygadenus venenosus, 34

About the Author

J. Duane Sept is a biologist, professional photographer and writer residing on the Sunshine Coast of British Columbia. His work has taken him to many areas throughout the Pacific Northwest. As a former interpreter or park naturalist he regularly shared a wealth of information with the public. Now he uses his photography to share the natural world he loves with people around the world.

Duane's images have appeared in *Canadian Wildlife, B.B.C. Wildlife, Nature Canada, Ranger Rick, Reader's Digest* and many more. He is also the author of THE BEACHCOMBER'S GUIDE TO SEASHORE LIFE IN THE PACIFIC NORTHWEST (Harbour Publishing) and THE BEACHCOMBER'S GUIDE TO SEASHORE LIFE OF CALIFORNIA (Harbour Publishing).